ENGLISH G

5

HEADLIGHT

Grammarmaster

Cornelsen

Headlight 5 – Grammarmaster

Erarbeitet von:
Gwen Berwick, York

sowie auf Grundlage von Arbeitsheften von:
Zoe Thorne, Brighton

in Zusammenarbeit mit der Englischredaktion:
Klaus Unger (Projektleitung), Lisa Ahmadi, Katrin Heinecke, Angela Obers, Anja Zieschang

Umschlaggestaltung:
Klein & Halm Grafikdesign, Berlin

Layoutkonzept:
Yvonne Thron (designcollective, Team für Mediengestaltung, Berlin)

Layout und technische Umsetzung:
Straive

www.cornelsen.de

1. Auflage, 1. Druck 2021

Druck: Athesiadruck GmbH

ISBN 978-3-06-036260-8

Inhalt

Life down under

Wiederholung: Das *simple present* und das *present progressive* SB pp. 182/183

Du verwendest das *simple present* für alles, was **regelmäßig** stattfindet (wie Gewohnheiten oder Hobbys) und für alles, was **immer** so ist. Du benutzt oft die Wörter *always, never, often, sometimes, usually, on Fridays* mit dem *simple present*.

On Sundays, Mum **visits** Grandma and I **go** with her. Dad **doesn't come**.

Du verwendest das *present progressive* für alles, was **gerade im Gang** (noch nicht abgeschlossen) ist oder um ein **Bild zu beschreiben**. Du benutzt oft die Wörter *at the moment, now, today* mit dem *present progressive*.

What **are** you **doing** at the moment? – **I'm making** a paper plane.

! He isn't going. They aren't going. Aber: I'm not going.

1 An interview on the beach

Write the sentences using the simple present or present progressive.

Tara: This afternoon, I am visiting (visit) the beach. Most people here are having (have) fun, but Mel is different. She isn't just playing (not just play) in the sand. Actually, she comes (come) here often. What are you doing (you / do) here today, Mel?

Mel: I am not playing (not play) – I am training (train)! I come (come) here most days to train.

Tara: What sport do you play (you / play) when you come here?

Mel: I play (play) beach volleyball. My partner Ali is over there, look – she is running (run) along the beach.

Tara: How often do you practise (you / practise)?

Mel: We practise (practise) for hours every day, but we don't train (not train) outside if it's too wet – we go (go) to the gym. At the moment, we are preparing (prepare) for the next Olympics.

Wiederholung: Das *going to-future* und das *will-future* SB p. 187

Das Futur mit ***going to*** wird verwendet,

- um über Vorhaben und Pläne für die Zukunft zu sprechen:

  What **are** you **going to** do at the weekend? – I**'m going to** go hiking with my dad.

- um auszudrücken, dass etwas gleich geschehen wird, weil es bereits Anzeichen dafür gibt:

  Look at those black clouds. It**'s going to** rain!

Das Futur mit ***will*** wird verwendet, um über die Zukunft zu sprechen. Es geht oft um

- Vermutungen oder Vorhersagen: I'm sure you**'ll feel** better tomorrow.
- Dinge, die wir nicht beeinflussen können:

  Will Christmas **be** on a Thursday next year?

- Spontane Hilfsangebote oder Versprechen:

  You don't look well. Do you know what? I **won't go** to the party. I**'ll stay** here with you.

2 Saying goodbye

Complete the sentences with *going to* + infinitive.

Mia: Do you know what? We are going to move (move) to South Australia in summer.

Miro: To South Australia? Why are you going to do (do) that?

Mia: Because my dad has a new job. He is going to help (help) to build a new wind farm.

Miro: Oh! And where are you going to go (go) to school?

Mia: I don't know yet. Dad says he is going to ask (ask) some of his colleagues[1] about schools there.

Miro: Oh dear. I'm going to miss (miss) you, Mia.

Mia: Me too, Miro. But we can keep in contact. We are going to videochat (video-chat) every week. And you are going to visit (visit) me in the holidays.

Miro: Yes, let's do that!

[1] **colleague** *(Arbeits-)Kollege*

3 A new wind farm in South Australia

Complete the sentences with *will* or *won't*.

To achieve its goal of using only renewable energy[2] by 2030, Australia has a number of onshore wind farms.[3] When it is finished, Carmody's Hill wind farm in South Australia **1** ________________ be one of four wind farms in that area. Building the wind farm **2** ________________ take 18 months. How much electricity **3** ________________ the new field make? We **4** ________________ know the answer till we know how big the new wind turbines[4] **5** ________________ be. 8.5% of Australia's electricity came from wind farms in 2019 and it is hoped that this **6** ________________ continue to go up. The result, of course, is that, in the future, Australia **7** ________________ need as much coal[5] and gas as it does now.

[2] **renewable energy** *erneuerbare Energien* [3] **onshore wind farm** *Windpark an Land* [4] **wind turbine** *Windrad, Windkraftanlage* [5] **coal** *Kohle*

4 Snow!

Complete the sentences with *will* or *going to*.

Wiederholung: Das *simple past* und das *present perfect* SB *pp. 183, 185*

Mit dem *simple past* sagst du, wann etwas in der Vergangenheit passiert ist:

I **went** there last year.

Mit dem *present perfect* drückst du aus, dass etwas in der Vergangenheit geschehen ist – der genaue Zeitpunkt ist dabei unwichtig oder nicht bekannt. Oft haben die Handlungen auch Auswirkungen auf die Gegenwart:

Have you ever **been** to Sydney? – **I've been** there three times.

5 In the summer holidays

Lucy is asking her friend Jack about his last holidays. Write her questions in the simple past.

1 what / you / do / in the holidays? What did ______________________

2 you / have / a good time? ______________________

3 who / you / go / with? ______________________

4 you / visit / Uluru? ______________________

5 you / bring / me a present? ______________________

6 Feelings

Complete the sentences with the correct form of the verbs. Use the present perfect.

1 Miro is tired. He ______________________ (clean) the kitchen and the bathroom.

2 Lisa and Ray are excited. They ______________________ (never be) to a live concert.

3 I'm scared: our neighbours ______________________ (buy) a really big dog.

4 Mr Robert is angry because someone ______________________ (break) his window.

5 Zonia feels nervous because she ______________________ (not work) hard enough for her test.

6 Koen feels lonely. He ______________________ (not talk) to anyone all afternoon.

Wiederholung: Das *past perfect* SB *pp. 186*

Mit dem *past perfect* drückst du aus, dass eine Handlung **vor einer anderen Handlung** oder **vor einem bestimmten Zeitpunkt in der Vergangenheit** stattfand. Das *past perfect* steht daher meist in einem Nebensatz; im zugehörigen Hauptsatz wird das *simple past* benutzt:

After the film **had ended**, I made a sandwich because I **hadn't eaten** any dinner.

7 Not a good day for Kylie

Read sentences 1–5. Decide what happened first and what happened after that. Write it in the table.

1 Kylie **(a) got up** after her parents **(b) had left** their house.

2 As soon as she **(a) had fed** her cats, she **(b) rode her bike** into town to meet her friends at their favourite cafe.

3 But her friends **(a) had already gone** to the shopping centre in King Street, so she **(b) left** the cafe and walked the short way to King Street.

4 At the shopping centre, she **(a) realized** that she **(b) had left** her bike outside the cafe.

5 She **(a) ran** back to the cafe, but someone **(b) had stolen** her bike.

	first	after that
1	b	a
2		
3		
4		
5		

8 Visiting Aunt Jane

What had Aunt Jane done before Jack and his mother arrived? Complete the verbs in the past perfect. Write the answers in the crossword.

1 Jane hadn't ... (forget) anything!

2 When we got to Jane's house, my aunt had ... (buy) flowers for Mum.

3 She had ... (make) a special cake.

4 And she had ... (cook) us a great meal too.

5 She had even ... (find) old photos of her and Mum.

6 She had ... (do) lots of other nice things.

7 She had even ... (put) balloons[6] on the door.

8 And she had ... (invite) some friends for a party.

[6] **balloon** *Luftballon*

9 An interview

Read Tara's interview with the owner of a gym. Write the correct forms of the verbs in brackets in the **simple present, present progressive, simple past** or **past perfect**.

Tara: Today I ______________ (talk) to Krish. He ______________ (own) a gym here in Sydney. ______________ ______________ (how many members / your gym / have), Krish?

Krish: My gym ______________ (have) about 3,000 members, although most members ______________ (not come) regularly. For example, lots of people ______________ (join) the gym last January – maybe because friends ______________ (give) them a membership[7] for Christmas. Most of those new members ______________ (come) only once or twice in January and then they ______________ (stop). Perhaps they ______________ (not really want) a membership. About 600 of our members ______________ (use) the gym almost every week. At the moment, ten people ______________ (do) Zumba over there. The teacher ______________ (teach) yoga every week too.

Tara: ______________ (when / you / open) the gym, Krish?

Krish: I opened the gym when I ______________ (move) to Australia 18 years ago. When I ______________ (grow up) in India, I often ______________ (dream) of living here.

Tara: ______________ (you / train) a lot when you lived in India?

Krish: I ______________ (not / train) at a gym. But one day, I ______________ (see) people at a gym on TV. I ______________ (think): "I ______________ (want) to do that!" That TV programme ______________ (change) my life!

[7] **membership** *Mitgliedschaft*

Respect

Wiederholung: Die indirekte Rede *(Indirect speech)*: Aussagen SB *pp.40, 192/193*

Wenn wir wörtlich wiedergeben, was jemand gesagt hat, verwenden wir die **direkte Rede** mit Anführungszeichen: Ruby said "I like you."

Wenn wir berichten, was jemand sagt, schreibt oder denkt, verwenden wir die **indirekte Rede** (ohne Anführungszeichen): Ruby told me (that) she liked me.

Veränderung der Zeitformen *(backshift of tenses)*: Ist das einleitende Verb *(told)* im *simple past*, wird in der indirekten Rede *simple present (like)* zu *simple past (liked)*.

Neben den Verben werden häufig auch **Pronomen** (*me, her, them* usw.) und **Possessivbegleiter** (*my, her, their* usw.) verändert.

Die **Wortstellung** ist Subjekt – Verb – ... Das Wort *that* („dass") wird oft weggelassen.

1 A review

Read the review of a new game called 'New Hack'. Then tell a friend what the review said about the game. Complete the sentences below in indirect speech.

New Hack

All the game magazines really like this new game because it takes ideas from other games and uses them in new ways. The graphics are awesome and you experience a lot of action. It can be hard to play if you don't play games often, but it's worth buying because it gives you a good time.

1 The review said that all the magazines really ______________________ this new game.

2 It said that the game ______________________ ideas from other games and ______________________ them in new ways.

3 The writer of the review thought that the graphics ______________________ awesome.

4 And the writer claimed that players ______________________ a lot of action.

5 The review warned that it ______________________ hard to play if you ______________________ games often.

6 But to sum up, the writer's opinion was that it ______________________ worth buying this game because it ______________________ you a good time.

2 Hide-and-seek

You and your friends played hide-and-seek[1] with your little cousin Diya. Complete the sentences.

1 First Diya told me that she could see ________________.

2 Then she told Emily that she could see ________________.

3 She told Jon and Kiera that she could see ________________.

4 Last of all she told Harry that she could see ________________.

3 Respect in the digital world

a) At a show about the digital world you heard a young woman talk about being an influencer. Report what she said by changing the highlighted words to indirect speech.

1 I'm an influencer and I promote[2] products that I really like.
2 But in my opinion as an influencer I must respect my followers.
3 I always tell them when I'm paid to talk about something.

1 She said ________________ an influencer and ________________ products that ________________ really ________________.

2 She added that in ________ opinion as an influencer ____________ respect ____________ followers.

3 She said ____________ always ____________ them when ____________ paid to talk about something.

b) You also heard a young man in a wheelchair talk about his experiences. Read the sentences, then write what the man said in direct speech.

1 The man said that he used a digitally controlled wheelchair, but that wasn't his biggest problem.
2 He said his real problem was that people often talked to him very slowly as if he was stupid or deaf.
3 He said that when he went out with his sister, people didn't talk to him directly but asked his sister how he was feeling.

1 "________________ a digitally controlled wheelchair, but that ________________."

2 ____

____

3 ____

____

[1] **play hide-and-seek** *Verstecken spielen* [2] **promote** *hier: Werbung machen für*

Indirekte Rede *(Indirect speech)*: Fragen (1) SB *pp. 41, 193*

Auch bei indirekten Fragen erfolgt der *backshift of tenses*, wenn das einleitende Verb im ***simple past*** steht *(asked, wanted to know)*.

Die Wortstellung in indirekten Fragen ist wie in Aussagesätzen: Subjekt – Verb – ... Ist die direkte Frage eine Frage **ohne Fragewort** *(yes-no question)*, dann wird die indirekte Frage mit *if* oder *whether* (Deutsch: „ob") eingeleitet (ohne Komma):

„Do you buy lots of things online?" Sam asked his friend Amy.	Sam wanted to know **if** Amy bought lots of things online.
„Amina, did you watch the film last night?" I wanted to know.	I wanted to know **whether** Amina had watched the film the night before.

Wenn die direkte Frage **mit einem Fragewort** (*where? when? how?* usw.) beginnt, dann bleibt das Fragewort in der indirekten Frage erhalten:

„**Where** did you buy your hat?" Mum asked.	Mum asked **where** I had bought my hat.

4 A job interview

a) Natalie had an interview at a graphic design company. On the way she was so nervous that she tripped and fell. A man helped her. Write down what the man asked.

Are you OK? Do you need an ambulance? Have you broken your leg? Will you be able to walk?

1 The man asked whether Natalie ______ and if she ______

______.

2 He asked ______.

3 He wanted to know ______.

b) Read what Natalie told her boyfriend about the interview. Then write the four questions in direct speech.

They asked me what sort of graphics I liked best and where I had learned computer programming. They wanted to know when I would be able to start. And then they asked how much I had earned in my last job.

1 "What sort of graphics ______?"

2 "Where ______?"

3 "When ______?"

4 " ______?"

Die indirekte Rede *(Indirect speech)*: Fragen (2) SB *pp.41, 193*

Bei indirekten Fragen steht wie in der direkten Frage eine Präposition am Satzende:

"What job did Dan apply for?" Ari asked.	„Um welche Stelle hat Dan sich beworben?", fragte Ari.
Ari asked what job Dan had applied **for**.	Ari fragte, um welche Stelle Dan sich beworben habe.

5 Zendaya and her mum

Zendaya is telling you what her mother asked her before her digital detox. Put the words in the right order.

1 When I arrived home, my mum asked me (from / had / come back / where / I).

My mum asked me where I had come back from ______.

2 My mum asked me (had / been / who / to / I / talking).

My mum asked me ______.

3 She asked me (I / what / was / for / phone / my / checking).

She asked me ______.

4 Then she asked me (about / what / I / worried / was).

She asked me ______.

5 And she asked me (of / what / I / had / uploaded / photos).

And she asked me ______.

6 Then she asked me (had / about / written / I / what).

Then she asked me ______.

7 And then my mum asked me (which / I / on / was / social media platforms).

And then she asked me ______

______.

8 Then my mum asked me (with / who / I / go / out).

And then my mum asked me ______.

9 When I told her, she asked me (what / I / thinking / of / was) – a person like that!

She asked me ______.

Die indirekte Rede *(Indirect speech)*: Aufforderungen, Bitten, Ratschläge SB pp. 41, 194

Bitten, Aufforderungen und Ratschläge werden in der Regel mit der **Infinitiv-Form** wiedergegeben:
Bei **Auffordnungen: *tell*** *somebody* ***to do*** *something*:

"Don't do that!" my friend said. → My friend told me not to do that.

Bei **Bitten**: ***ask*** *somebody* ***to do*** *something*:

"Please pass me the jam," my sister said. → My sister asked me to pass her the jam.

Bei **Ratschlägen: *advise*** *somebody* ***to do*** *something*:

"I don't think you should go there," he said. → He advised me not to go there.

6 Good advice?

Tim has a date. He's nervous and has asked some friends for advice. Complete the sentences.

Amy: Talk about your interests.

Carl: Don't panic. Stay calm.

Max: Don't worry too much about your clothes. Wear something comfortable.

Cindy: Do something active. Don't meet in a cafe.

1 Amy advised me ______________ about my interests.

2 Carl advised me ______________ and ______________ calm.

3 Max advised me ______________ too much about my clothes and ______________ something comfortable.

4 Cindy advised me ______________ something active and ______________ in a café.

7 Tim's evening

Tim reports on how the evening went. Complete the sentences with one verb from box 1 for the first gap and one from box 2 for the second gap.

advise • ask • tell

come • meet • wear

1 Sam messaged me and ______________ me ______________ him in the New World Cafe.

2 I told him I'd rather go for a walk and ______________ him ______________ to the park instead.

3 Sam was dressed very smartly while I was wearing jeans and sneakers. I told him you had ______________ me ______________ something comfortable. He laughed.

Die indirekte Rede: Verschiebung der Zeitformen SB pp. 42, 193/194

Steht das einleitende Verb in der Vergangenheit, werden die Zeitformen der direkten Rede meist um eine Zeitstufe in die Vergangenheit „zurückverschoben“ *(backshift of tenses)*.

	Direkte Rede	Indirekte Rede: *Nav said (that) ...*
present progressive → past progressive	"**I'm** playing a new game."	he **was** playing a new game.
simple present → simple past	"I **check** my phone every day."	he **checked** his phone every day.
simple past → past perfect	"I **posted** photos of myself."	he **had** posted photos of himself.
present perfect → past perfect	"I **have** never tried a digital detox."	he **had** never tried a digital detox.
will → would *can → could*	"I **will** upload the film when I **can**."	he **would** upload the film when he **could**.
am/are/is going to → was/were going to	"I **am** not going to shut my account."	he **was** not going to shut his account.

8 A survey about social media

Read what these students said about social media. Use indirect speech.

1 Mohammed: "I don't need social media to keep in touch with my friends."

Mohammed said that ______________________ social media to keep in touch with ______________________ friends.

2 Lukas: "In my opinion, social media have saved lives after many accidents."

Lukas said in ______________________ opinion social media ______________________ lives after many accidents.

3 Hannah: "I hope social media will help me to make new friends."

Hannah said ______________________ social media ______________________ to make new friends.

4 Sophia: "I began to use social media at primary school."

Sophia said ______________________ to use social media at primary school.

5 Felix: "I'm sure social media are going to influence our lives more and more."

Felix ______________________ sure social media ______________________ to influence our lives more and more.

6 Radhia: "I think social media platforms are getting better."

Radhia ______________________ social media platforms ______________________ better.

Partizipialkonstruktionen SB pp. 52, 199

Partizipialkonstruktionen verwendet man vor allem im geschriebenen Englisch. Sie stehen **anstelle von Nebensätzen** und geben Informationen über die **Zeit**, den **Grund** oder die **Begleitumstände** einer Handlung.

Du verwendest in diesen Partizipialkonstruktionen das **Partizip Präsens** (*present participle*). Du kennst es schon von den Verlaufsformen.

Du bildest es so: Verb + *-ing*

While **running** down the street, I saw something strange.	= wann? (*While I was running down the street …*)
Feeling ill, he decided to stay in bed.	= warum? (*Because he felt ill …*)
William built a windmill **using** a bike.	= wie? (*William used a bike to build …*)

Steht die Partizipialkonstruktion **vor** dem Hauptsatz, kannst du die Konjunktion weglassen.

I saw something strange while **running** down the street.

Running down the street, I saw something strange.

More challenge 1 Strange ways

Many famous people do and did things in an unusual way. Complete the sentences with the **present participles** of the verbs in brackets.

★ ____________________ (wear) his shoes on his hands, writer William Faulkner wrote his books with his feet.

★ Ludwig van Beethoven often wrote music while ____________________ (have) a bath.

★ ____________________ (want) to finish his books on time, writer Victor Hugo did not leave his house until he was finished – even though they were often over 1,000 pages long!

★ Inventor Nikola Tesla said that he was in love with a bird that he found, ____________________ (take) it home to live with him.

★ Bill Gates programmes and has meetings while ____________________ (sit) in a special chair that moves.

★ Inventor Dr Yoshiro Nakamatsu thought of ideas for inventions while ____________________ (swim) underwater.

★ ____________________ (be) afraid of illness, actress Cameron Diaz opens doors with her elbows.

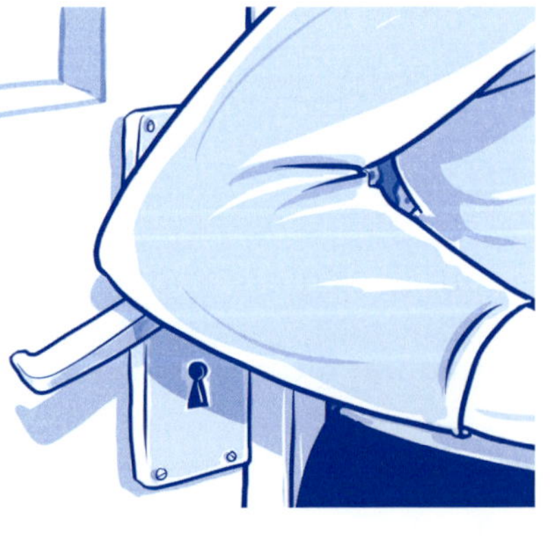

More challenge 2 A strange dream

a) Alex is writing about a very strange dream he had last night. Change the underlined phrases to a **participle construction**.

1 While I **walked** through a forest, I saw a deer.
While walking through a forest, I saw a deer.

2 While it **stood** on two legs, the deer smiled at me and said hello.

3 Because I **am** polite, I said hello back even though I was confused.

4 Then I saw a bird that **flew** through the forest and **sang** my favourite song.

5 When I **ran** towards the bird, I fell over.

6 As I **fell** to the floor, I called the deer to help me.

b) Alex is writing more about his dream. Change the sentences, so that they use a **participle construction**.

1 Because she wanted to talk to me, my teacher suddenly arrived.

2 When she heard that I hadn't done my homework, she looked angry.

3 When I got up, I found a Christmas present.

4 When I gave the present to my teacher, I told her that it was my homework.

5 As she took the present from me, she smiled.

Looking forward

Wortstellung in Aussagen (1) SB pp. 66, 188

In Aussagesätzen gilt immer die Regel ***subject – verb – object*** (S-V-O).

	Subjekt	Verb	Objekt		Subjekt	Verb	
	I	play	tennis.				
Yesterday	I	didn't play	tennis	because	I	was	too tired.

Adverbien der Zeit und Häufigkeit (*already, just, never, often*) stehen **vor** einem *past participle.*

I have **never** played tennis.

Die Adverbien, die dem ganzen Satz den Ton geben (*luckily, unfortunately*) stehen meist am **Satzanfang**.

Unfortunately, I can't play the guitar.

Adverbien, die sich auf ein Verb bzw. eine Tätigkeit beziehen, stehen meist am Satzende.

After her date with Ben, Lia walked home **happily**.

1 You are the teacher

A German student has tried to describe the picture. In each sentence ONE WORD is in the WRONG place. Cross out this word and write the correct sentence for the student.

1 In the photo ~~can~~ I see a tent.

____

2 Two people have started already cooking.

____

3 Unfortunately, has it just started to rain.

____

4 We stay always in a hotel when we go away.

____

5 So I have been never camping.

____

6 But of course I think it could fun be.

____

Wortstellung in Aussagen (2) SB *pp. 66, 188*

Gibt es in einem Satz eine Orts- und eine Zeitangabe, gilt die Regel: **Ort** vor **Zeit**.

Ben met Li **at the youth club three weeks ago**.

2 A festival of world music

You and your friend Julian are at a festival of world music, and you meet some young South Africans. Mediate for Julian. Complete the sentences.

1. Vor zwei Jahren habe ich eine südafrikanische Band bei einem Konzert in Berlin gehört.

   I heard a South African band at a concert ______

2. Und ich bin ein paar Monate später auf dieses Festival hier in Berlin gegangen.

   And I went to this festival ______

3. Jetzt komme ich jedes Jahr hierher.

   Now I come ______

4. Am Freitag habe ich hier eine tolle Band aus Cape Town gehört.

   I heard a great band from Cape Town ______

5. Nun möchte ich gern nächstes Jahr nach Südafrika reisen.

   Now I'd like to travel ______

3 A new job

Put the words in brackets in the right order to complete the sentences.

1 I was happy ______

(when / I / my / part-time job / got)

2 On the first day ______

(nervously / I / there / walked)

3 I got to know ______

(quickly / my / colleagues / very)

4 Now we often ______

(after / cafe / meet / work / in / a)

Wortstellung in Fragesätzen SB *pp. 66, 189*

In Fragesätzen verwendet man das Hilfsverb *do/does* im *simple present* und *did* im *simple past*. Das Vollverb steht im Infinitiv (*feel, play, swim*). Bei der 3. Person Singular braucht das Vollverb kein *-s*, denn es steckt schon in *does*.

In Fragesätzen steht das Hilfsverb vor dem Subjekt. Das Vollverb steht – wie im Aussagesatz – nach dem Subjekt. Fragewörter stehen – wie im Deutschen – am Anfang des Satzes.

Fragewort	Hilfsverb	Subjekt	Vollverb	Objekt	
	Does	your friend	start	a new job	tomorrow?
Where	do	you	start	your new job?	

In Fragen mit *be* wird das Hilfsverb *do* **nicht** verwendet. **Is** your friend reliable?

4 Questions at an interview

Read the interview for a new job. Fill the gaps with question words from the box.

how • how many • how much • when • where • who • why

Employer: Good morning. Please sit down. I'm going to ask you a few questions. First of all, ____________ old are you?

Candidate: I'm 17.

Employer: You said you had a part-time job. ____________ do you work?

Candidate: In the cake shop in Sheep Street.

Employer: And ____________ hours a week do you work there?

Candidate: Four hours on Saturday, and sometimes more in the holidays.

Employer: And ____________ do you earn per hour?

Candidate: The minimum wage[1].

Employer: And can you tell me please: ____________ do you want to change jobs?

Candidate: I'd like to earn a bit more money.

Employer: And ____________ could you start working with us?

Candidate: I could start in two weeks.

Employer: That sounds all right. Oh, ____________ is your boss in the shop?

Candidate: Ms Reed.

Employer: I'll need to contact her of course. ...

[1] **minimum wage** *Mindestlohn*

5 The Edinburgh Fringe Festival

a) Read the text about the Edinburgh Fringe Festival.

The Edinburgh Fringe Festival

Are you looking for something bigger, something better in life?

Then the Edinburgh Fringe Festival is for you. It is quite simply the biggest arts festival in the world: in 2018 it put on over 3500 different shows in 25 days, in schools, theatres, pubs, church halls, conference centres, hotels, even in a bus and in the back of a taxi. Only the Olympic Games and the Football World Cup sell more tickets than the Edinburgh Fringe!

Do you know the British comedian Rowan Atkinson, who plays Mr Bean? He is just one of many actors who began their careers at the Edinburgh Fringe Festival. Most shows have ticket prices, but the prices are low because there is so much competition. But some shows are free and ask you to pay as much as you want when you leave the show.

The festival has taken place every August since 1947, except in 2020 when it couldn't open because of the Covid pandemic.

b) Complete the questions about the festival. Be careful: think about which tense you need.

c) EXTRA: Then read the text again and write short answers.

1 When ________ the Edinburgh Fringe Festival put on its first show? – In ________

2 In which month ________ the festival always take place? – In ________

3 ________ you have to pay for the tickets? – ________

4 Over how many days ________ the festival take place in 2018? – ________

5 And how many shows ________ the festival put on in 2018? – ________

6 ________ the Edinburgh Fringe Festival usually sell more tickets than the Olympic Games? – ________

7 Where ________ the shows take place? – In many different ________

8 Why ________ no shows take place in 2020? – Because of the ________

6 Food: are you boring or brave?

a) Write questions for a personality test in a magazine about food. Put the words in the right order.

1 you / can / cook / ?

____

2 do / in a restaurant / what / usually order / you / ?

____

3 hate / types of food / how many / you / do / ?

____

4 like to try / when you are on holiday / you / the local food / do / ?

____

b) Match the questions from a) with the answers and write the correct number.

a ____________

A *No way. I always try to find a burger restaurant.*

B *Sometimes, if I know I like what they have, and it's not too expensive.*

C *Of course! That's one of the best things about travelling! It's exciting to try something new.*

b ____________

A *Putting a pizza in the microwave is cooking, right?*

B *I know easy things to cook.*

C *I collect recipes from around the world and I love trying them.*

c ____________

A *Hundreds! I don't like most vegetables, or nuts, and I don't really like cheese or yoghurt.*

B *One or two, like most people*

C *Let me see ... No, I can't think of any food that I don't like.*

d ____________

A *I always order the same thing. I don't like surprises.*

B *I like to try different dishes sometimes, but of course I have my favourites.*

C *I always choose the special of the day. That way I eat dishes that I would never think of ordering.*

c) Do the test yourself. Check how many As, Bs or Cs you have. Then look at the answers on the right and find out how boring or brave you are with food.

Mostly A: You know what you like to eat and you don't like to try anything else. But doesn't it get boring sometimes? Why not try something exciting now and then? You might really like it!
Mostly B: You sometimes try new dishes, as long as they are not too different. You could be a little braver sometimes.
Mostly C: Wow, you love exciting food, don't you? What will you try next?

7 Messaging a friend

Last week you met a nice guy called Dan who was staying with his cousin in Germany. Now Dan is back home in Edinburgh, and you message him.

Write questions. Be careful. Think about:

- which verb you need: *be* or *do/did*
- which tense you need
- if you need a question word

Hi, Dan, I hope you're OK.

1 (you / have / a good trip / back to Edinburgh / ?)

____

2 (your plane / on time / ?)

____

3 I hope you had a great time here in Germany. (German food / you / like best / ?)

____

4 My favourite place near here is the castle. (your cousin / take you there / ?)

____

5 We have a strong accent in this part of Germany. So I wonder – (you / always / able to understand / us / ?)

____

6 (you / want to come / again / next year / ?)

____

I hope so. It was nice meeting you.

Fragen im Passiv SB pp. 125, 190

Fragen im Passiv bildest du mit ***be + past participle***:

Fragewort	***be***	**Subjekt**	***past participle***	
	Was	James	**hurt**	in the accident?
Where	**was**	he	**hurt**?	

8 A quiz

a) Write the correct past tense verb. Then write your answer to each question.

1 ____________ the Eiffel Tower built in 1789 or 1889? ________________

2 ____________ the Harry Potter books written by a man or a woman? ________________

3 ____________ the book *Oliver Twist* written in 1838 or 1938? ________________

4 ____________ carrots brought to Europe from Turkey or America? ________________

b) Write the correct past tense verb and past participle of the verb in brackets. Then circle the right answer.

1 When ________________ penicillin ________________ (discover)?

1728 1828 1928

2 Where ________________ women first ________________ (give) the right to vote?

England USA New Zealand

3 Where ________________ the world's first football league ________________ (found)?

France England Spain

c) Write the correct present tense verb and past participle of the verb in brackets. Then circle the right answer.

1 Which US city ________________________________ (know) as the Big Apple?

San Francisco New York Miami

2 Which language ________________________________ (speak) by most people in the world?

French Chinese English

3 Where ________________ most films ________________ (make)?

India Russia USA

d) Now check your answers on page 58.

Fragen mit Modalverben SB pp. 125, 190

Ja/Nein-Fragen mit *modals* beginnen mit dem Modalverb. Das Hilfsverb *do* wird **nicht** verwendet.

Brauchst du auch ein Fragewort, steht dieses noch vor dem Modalverb.

Fragewort	Modalverb	Subjekt	Vollverb	
	May	I	go out	this evening, Dad?
What time	**must**	I	come	home?

9 Looking for a new flat

Kinga is looking for a new flat. Write her questions.

Can / pets have / I / ?

I / quiet / must / after / 10 pm / be / ?

my ukulele / play / I / may / ?

take / I / should / this flat / ?

1 ______

2 ______

3 ______

4 ______

10 At the railway station

Hamza is travelling from Birmingham to York. Write questions using the words in brackets.

Woman: Good morning. (can / how / you / help / I / ?)

______

Hamza: I'd like a ticket for the 9.53 train to York, please. (it / when / arrive / will / in York / ?)

______

Woman: At 12.25.

Hamza: OK, thanks. (may / I / on the train / my bike / take / ?)

______

Woman: Yes, of course.

Hamza: And I'd like to have a coffee. (should / I / buy / it / where / ?)

______

Woman: You can buy really nice coffee on the train.

Subjekt- und Objektfragen

SB pp. 125, 189

a) Fragen nach dem Subjekt

Fragt man nach dem Subjekt eines Aussagesatzes, (Frage: „Wer oder was?“), braucht man kein Hilfsverb, da das Fragewort das Subjekt ersetzt. Dies ist sehr häufig bei den Fragewörtern *who, which* und *what* der Fall. Die Wortstellung ist wie im Aussagesatz:

Fragewort (= Subjekt)	Vollverb	
Who	was	the first man on the moon?
(Neil Armstrong	*was*	*the first man on the moon.)*
What	has	eight legs and scares people?
(Spiders	*have*	*eight legs and scare people.)*

Das ist im Deutschen genauso.

b) Fragen nach dem Objekt

Fragen nach dem Objekt eines Aussagesatzes bildet man mit einem Hilfsverb, z.B. *do/does/did.*

Fragewort (= Objekt)	Hilfsverb	Subjekt	Vollverb	
Who	did	you	see	yesterday?
(You saw a famous person yesterday)				
What	does	she	like?	
(She likes music.)				

More challenge 1 Noises in the night

Complete the dialogue using the verbs in the box in the simple past.

be • happen • scare • work

Ben: I was scared last night.

Rosh: What ______________ you?

Ben: A loud noise.

Rosh: What ______________ then?

Ben: I switched on my phone. That worked.

Rosh: What do you mean? What ______________?

Ben: I watched a good film. And I fell asleep. But then I heard a loud noise again!

Rosh: Oh no! What ______________ it?

Ben: My alarm clock.

More challenge 2 **A rap**

In this rap called "Questions", Idris has written about his experiences as a Muslim American in New York, but the rap speaks to any person who feels that he or she is somehow a bit different.

a) The rap has many object questions. For each question, choose a verb from the box. You will need some of the verbs more than once, and sometimes more than one verb could be right.

do • does • did • will • were • would • can • could • must

Hey businessman, going about your day

Who moved when I sat next to you on the subway.

What ________ you think I was going to do?

What ________ you scared of? That I would hurt you?

Just because I don't look like you.

What ________ it take to make you understand that I'm a New Yorker too?

Man, are you for real?

What ________ it feel like to know you'll never fit in?

What ________ your life be like in my skin?

What ________ you think when you look at me?

Tell me, what ________ you see?

Your mind is so narrow – what ________ I do to open it wider?

What ________ I say to show you I'm not an outsider?

Who ________ you think you are?

What ________ you say when I'm a star?

When everyone wants a selfie with me,

Will you finally agree

I belong in NYC?

b) Write suitable verbs in these questions about the rap. Then answer the questions.

1 Who ________ away when Idris sat in the subway? – A ________.

2 How ________ Idris feel that he is different? – He ________

____

3 What ________ Idris say he will be later in life? – A ________.

Fragen mit Fragewörtern und Präpositionen SB pp. 126, 190

Präpositionen stehen vor Nomen (***after** lunch, **with** my friends*) und kommen oft in Wendungen mit Verben vor (*look **at**, wait **for**, fit **in with***).

Wenn du **Fragen mit Präpositionen** bildest, stehen

- die **Fragewörter** am **Anfang** der Frage.
- die **Präpositionen** am **Ende** der Frage.

Vorsicht: das ist anders als im Deutschen, wo die Präpositionen meist vor dem Fragewort stehen oder ein neues Fragewort mit *wo-* beginnt.

Fragewort		**Präposition**	
Who	did he walk	**with**?	(Mit wem ging er spazieren?)
Which	team do you play	**for**?	(Für welche Mannschaft spielst du?)
What	are you looking	**forward to**?	(Worauf freust du dich?)

More challenge 3 Stopped by the police

One evening a police officer stops you and asks you questions. Write the prepositions. You won't need all of the prepositions in the box.

about • after • at • before • near • for • in • of • till • to • with

1 What were you looking ______?
2 What were you waiting ______?
3 What were you frightened ______?
4 Which restaurant had you eaten ______?
5 When were you there ______?
6 What were you talking ______?
7 Who do you live ______?
8 Which school do you go ______?

More challenge 4 Questions to a new friend

Put the words in the right order and write questions.

1 (in / which / town / you / live / do / ?) ______
2 (live / you / do / who / with / ?) ______
3 (do / about / what / dream / you / ?) ______

More challenge 5 Looking for a new job

Lalita has a job in a shop, but is looking for a new job. She's at a job interview. Look at her answers. Then complete the employer's questions. Tip: Use the verb and preposition from the answer.

1 **Employer:** Which school ______________________________?

Lalita: I go to Kent School.

2 **Employer:** What sort of shop ______________________________?

Lalita: I work in a flower shop.

3 **Employer:** What sort of ______________________________?

Lalita: I'm looking for an office job.

4 **Employer:** When ______________________________?

Lalita: I can start from Monday 15th May.

More challenge 6 Mediation

You're at a party with your friend Jens, and you meet a girl from Australia who is working in a hospital in town. Jens fancies her, but is too shy to ask questions in English. Mediate for him and write questions in English using the words in the box.

be to • come from • look after • stay with • work in • look forward to

1 **Jens:** Woher kommst du?

You: ______________________________?

2 **Jens:** Bei wem wohnst du?

You: ______________________________?

3 **Jens:** An welchen Orten hier in der Nähe bist du gewesen?

You: ______________________________?

4 **Jens:** In welchem Krankenhaus arbeitest du?

You: ______________________________?

5 **Jens:** Um welche Menschen kümmerst du dich?

You: ______________________________?

6 **Jens:** Worauf freust du dich, wenn du zurück in Australien bist?

You: ______________________________?

Frageanhängsel (*Question tags*) SB pp. 67, 203

Question tags werden im Englischen **in Gesprächen** verwendet. Man benutzt sie,

- um **Zustimmung** zu erreichen.
- als echte **Nachfrage**, wenn man unsicher ist.

Die englischen *question tags* entsprechen gell?/oder?/nicht wahr?/ne? im Deutschen.

Bildung der Frageanhängsel
Die *question tags* richten sich nach dem **Verb** und nach der **Person** im Satz.

- Bei *be* und Modalverben wird das Verb verneint (ein negatives Verb wird bejaht).
- Bei Vollverben *(play, work, eat)* wird die Verneinung durch *don't/doesn't* bzw. *didn't* gezeigt, die Bejahung durch *do/does* bzw. *did*
- Die Person bleibt gleich. Personennamen (Jack, Sara) werden durch Pronomen *(he, she)* ersetzt.

Bejahter Satz + verneintes Frageanhängsel	Verneinter Satz + bejahtes Frageanhängsel
Noah **is** angry, **isn't** he?	You **aren't** going to leave, **are** you?
It'**s** raining, **isn't** it?	Ellie **isn't** ill, **is** she?
There **is** a cat in the garden, **isn't** there?	I **won't** finish my work in time, **will** I?
We **can** win, **can't** we?	We **mustn't** go there, **must** we?
They **live** in Manchester, **don't** they?	You **don't work** here, **do** you?

11 Thoughts in a club

Lilly is getting a bit tired of her boyfriend Lawson. She sees a good-looking boy at a dance. Read her thoughts, then circle the right question tag.

1. That boy Alek is Polish, is he? / isn't he?
2. He doesn't live here, does he? / doesn't he?
3. But he can dance well, can he? / can't he?
4. And he really likes dancing, does he? / doesn't he?
5. Well, I'm not shy, am I? / aren't I?
6. So I can ask him to dance with me, can I? / can't I?
7. Alek! Alek! Oh dear, the music is too loud! He can't hear me, can he? / can't he?
8. I'll have to dance with Lawson after all, will I? / won't I?

12 In a new flat

Ibrahim and Celina are excited because they have just moved into a new flat. They can't stop talking about it!

a) Read their sentences and use the right form of the verb *be* in your question tags.

1 The flat is great, ______ it?

2 Our new neighbours are nice, ______ they?

3 They brought some tea and biscuits. That was really kind, ______ it?

4 The rooms aren't very big, ______ they?

5 There isn't any room for the wardrobe, ______ there?

6 But we're very happy here, ______ we?

b) Now use the right question tag with *do* from the box.

did we? • didn't we? • doesn't it? • does it? • do we? • don't they?

1 The big sofa looks good over there, ______?

2 We only just got it through the front door, ______?

3 The curtains go well with the carpet, ______?

4 The noise from the street doesn't matter, ______?

5 We didn't have any big problems, ______?

6 But we don't want to move again for a long time now, ______?

13 Rugby: a game with strange rules

Marcus isn't very sure about the rules of rugby. Write the question tags.

1 There are fifteen players in a team, ______?

2 You use a ball that isn't round, ______?

3 It isn't a summer sport, ______?

4 You can hold the ball in your hands, ______?

5 But you can't pass the ball forwards, ______?

6 You don't score by kicking the ball into a goal, ______?

7 It's a popular sport in Wales, ______?

8 You must try to stop the other players, ______?

Generation *like*

Wiederholung: Bedingungssätze, Typ 1 (1) SB p. 196

Mit Bedingungssätzen vom Typ 1 drückst du aus, was unter bestimmten Bedingungen passieren kann oder passieren wird. Sie bestehen aus zwei Teilsätzen: Die Bedingung steht im *if*-Satz (Nebensatz). Das Verb steht hier im *simple present*. Der Hauptsatz beschreibt, was folgt, wenn die Bedingung erfüllt wird. Das Verb steht meist im *will-future*.

if-Nebensatz (Bedingung): ***simple present***	Hauptsatz (Folge): ***will-future***
If they **come** early,	I'**ll be** surprised.

Der *if*-Satz kann vor oder nach dem Hauptsatz stehen. Anders als im Deutschen setzt man **kein** Komma, wenn der *if*-Satz am Ende steht.

We won't be in trouble if they don't see us.

1 Have you heard this before?

Here are some well-known fears about social media. Complete the sentences using the verbs in brackets in the right form.

1 If you ______________ (play) too many games, you ______________ (get) addicted.

2 Your eyes ______________ (get) worse if you ______________ (watch) the screen too long.

3 Your school work ______________ (suffer) if you ______________ (use) your phone at school.

4 If you ______________ (use) your phone in bed, you ______________ (not get) enough sleep.

5 If you ______________ (use) social media, people ______________ (know) everything about you.

6 People ______________ (not be) able to read books if they ______________ (watch) their screens all day.

Wiederholung: Bedingungssätze, Typ 1 (2) SB *p. 196*

In Bedingungssätzen können im **Hauptsatz** statt *will-future* auch stehen:

- **Modalverb (*can/must/should*):**

If you need help, you **can/must/should** call me.

- **Imperativ:**

If you need help, **call** me.

2 Good advice for using social media

Give good advice for using social media. Use the sentence parts. Write ONE sentence each with *can/can't, must/mustn't, should/shouldn't* and the imperative.

★ (if you / use / social media / choose / your friends carefully)

★ (not tell / your friends / if you / have / a secret)

★ (if you / be / busy / answer / your messages later)

★ (not answer / a message / if you / not know / who sent it)

★ ____

____

★ ____

____

★ ____

____

★ ____

____

Wiederholung: Bedingungssätze, Typ 2 SB p. 197

Bedingungssätze vom Typ 2 beschreiben, was unter bestimmten Bedingungen passieren würde. „Was wäre, wenn ..." Der Nebensatz mit *if* beschreibt oft eine **unwahrscheinliche oder unsichere Bedingung**. Im Hauptsatz steht, was in diesem Fall passieren würde. Im Deutschen verwendet man hier oft würde/wäre/hätte.

if-Nebensatz: ***simple past***	Hauptsatz: ***would/wouldn't / could/couldn't / might (not)***
If my parents **gave** me some money,	I **would buy** a new phone.
If I **had** an older phone,	I **couldn't watch** films on it.
If I **didn't have** a phone,	I **might go** mad.

3 Without my phone for a week

Imagine you couldn't use your phone for a week. How would you feel? Complete the sentences using the verbs in brackets. Use the correct forms for if-sentences type 2.

If I ____________ (not have) my phone for a week, I think I ____________ (not know) what to do! I think I ____________ (feel) lonely if I ____________ (not chat) with my friends. And my homework ____________ (be) harder if I ____________ (not able to go) online. But on the other hand I ____________ (might spend) more time with my dog. And if we ____________ (go) for a long walk together, we ____________ (have) good fun.

4 Not always what you think

Read what these two teenagers say about themselves. Circle the right form of the verbs. Then underline the one if-sentence type 1.

If you saw / would see me with my friends, you imagined / would imagine that I'm a confident teenager who loves sharing pictures of myself. Some of my friends didn't care / wouldn't care if their photos were shown / would be shown on the internet. But I hated / would hate it if people showed / would show pictures of me. I'm really shy!

If you didn't know / wouldn't know me well, you guessed / would guess I'm a typical screenager. I bet you didn't believe / wouldn't believe me if I told / would tell you that I actually don't use my phone much. In fact, if you want / will want to find me after school, you see / 'll see me on a sports field – but definitely not on my phone!

Bedingungssätze, Typ 3 SB pp. 89, 197

Mit *if*-Sätzen Typ 3 stellst du dir vor, was in der Vergangenheit unter bestimmten Bedingungen hätte geschehen können: „Was wäre gewesen, wenn ..."

if-Nebensatz:	Hauptsatz:
past perfect	***would/wouldn't have / could/couldn't have / might (not) have + past participle***
If my parents **had given** me some money,	I **would have bought** a new phone.
If I **had been** more careful,	I **might not have read** that new message.
If we **had shared** the information,	we **could have gone** to the concert together.

Die Kurzform sowohl von ***had*** als auch von ***would*** ist ***'d***.

If they**'d** stayed at home, they'**d** have missed a good film at the cinema.

5 If we had known ...

a) An online magazine asked readers what, looking back, they might have done differently in their lives, and why. Read and match the sentence halves: Write A-F in the boxes below.

1 If I had known that children in poor countries make lots of our cheap jeans and T-shirts, ☐	**4** If I had known how much discrimination there is against people of colour, ☐
2 If we had thought more deeply about the damage that plastic does in the ocean, ☐	**5** If I had known some of the horrible things that people can do online with photos, ☐
3 If I had known that so many people suffer so much from cyberbullying, ☐	**6** If I had realized how exciting online games are, ☐

A ... I would have been more careful with the language I use in my messages.	**D** ... we would have bought fewer drinks in plastic bottles.
B ... I would have shared fewer pictures of myself on social media.	**E** ... I would have tried harder to make friends with students from different backgrounds.
C ... I would have bought my clothes in different shops.	**F** ... I would have learned to play more of them earlier.

b) Now complete the following sentences using the words in brackets.

1 If I had known that there are so many dangerous materials in phones, ______________________________

______________________________ (I / keep / my old phone / longer)

2 If I had known that flying causes so much air pollution, ______________________________

______________________________ (I / not fly / so often)

3 If I had seen the amazing work that some charities do, ______________________________

______________________________ (I / give / them / more money)

6 A special birthday activity

Seo-Yeon and her best friend went jet surfing. Read her diary entry and underline if-sentences type 1, type 2 and type 3 in three different colours.

I once told my best friend Aqila that if I had the choice of any activity for my birthday, I'd choose jet surfing. So, being the friend she is, Aqila booked an hour for us at the jet surfing centre on a lake outside our town. We planned to go there by bus, but one thing is true – if I have to get up early for something important, I won't hear my alarm. I slept too long – and we would never have arrived at the jet surfing centre in time if Aqila's mum hadn't driven us there.

But we had an amazing time, and if anyone asked me for a tip for a birthday, I'd definitely recommend jet surfing.

A jet surf is like a surf-board, with a motor. It isn't as easy as it looks. If our trainer hadn't helped me, I might never have been able even to stand! But after fifteen minutes or so I was OK on my own, and I loved controlling how fast I moved. I learned that if you go too fast, the surfboard will rise and you'll fall into the water.

It was an amazing experience. I'd happily have paid for a second hour if other people hadn't already booked it. So if we went again, I'd definitely book a longer time for the surfing.

My only problem now is that if Aqila asks me for a fun activity for her birthday, I'll have to think of something really good! Or if I can't think of anything else, maybe we will go jet surfing again!

7 What if?

a) Harry wrote a poem. Read his poem and (circle) the right form of the verbs.

If …

If I hadn't lost / wouldn't lose my phone that day,
my life had been / would have been so different.

My bus pass is on my phone,
so I had taken / would have taken the bus
if I had had / would have had my phone.

I had gone / would have gone by bike
If someone hadn't stolen / wouldn't have stolen it

I had asked / would have asked my dad to drive me into town
If I had had / would have had the chance to phone him

But instead I walked, feeling fed up because of the rain,
and thinking of all the calls I was missing

If I had known / would have known, I hadn't minded / wouldn't have minded.

Because if I hadn't walked / wouldn't have walked
You hadn't seen / wouldn't have seen me on the street.

If the weather had been / would have been good
You hadn't offered / wouldn't have offered to share your umbrella.

If we hadn't talked / wouldn't have talked for hours, forgetting where we were,
We hadn't fallen / wouldn't have fallen in love

I'm so glad I lost my phone that day …

b) Complete the sentences about the poem. Use the correct form of the verbs in brackets to form if-sentences, type 3.

1 If Harry ______________________ (not walk), he ______________________ (not meet) his future partner.

2 If his future partner ______________________ (go) a different way, they ______________________ (miss) each other.

3 And they ______________________ (not speak) to each other if Harry's future partner ______________________ (not bring) a big umbrella.

8 Lucky or unlucky?

a) Read the magazine article about an accident in the Lake District, a mountainous area in the north west of England.

Lucky escape

A climber had a lucky escape in the Lake District. Frank Smith was hiking alone when fog suddenly came down over the mountains. Soon Frank wasn't able to see the path, and then he slipped, fell off the path and broke his leg – and his phone. So he shouted for help, and luckily another hiker heard him and phoned the air ambulance service. Fortunately, the air ambulance service can use jet suits to save people on the mountains. Using a jet suit they can reach people much faster than when they had to walk up the mountain. So when they got the call, a member of the air ambulance service 'flew' to Frank and gave him first aid. She then phoned for a helicopter, and the helicopter was able to take Frank to hospital in Carlisle.

b) Complete the if-clauses in the type 3 conditional sentences.

1 If it ______________________ foggy, Frank would have been able to see the path.

2 If Frank ______________________ for help, nobody would have seen him.

3 If a hiker ______________________ him, Frank might have died of cold.

c) Now complete the main clauses in the type 3 conditional sentences.

4 If the hiker hadn't had a phone, he ______________________ for help.

5 If the air ambulance service hadn't used jet suits, they ______________________ Frank so quickly.

6 If they had had to walk up the mountain, they ______________________ much slower.

d) Now write the if-sentence, type 3.

7 (if the helicopter / not come, / Frank / not get / to hospital so quickly)

____

____

8 (if Frank / not go / to the Lake District that day, / he / not fall)

____

____

9 A Beatles fan

Johanna is a Beatles fan. Read her post.

a) Your challenge: Decide whether the if-sentences should be type 1, type 2 or type 3. Write "type 1", "type 2" or "type 3" in the box on the right.

b) Write the if-sentences.

1 I'm a real Beatles fan. (I / always **be** happy / if I / **hear** / one of their songs)

2 I often think: (If I / **be** / a teenager in the 1960s / I / **see** / the Beatles) But of course I wasn't, so I didn't.

3 Sometimes I dream of visiting Liverpool, where the Beatles grew up. Unfortunately, I don't earn much. (If I / **earn** / more / I / **book** / a flight to Liverpool at once)

4 It's bad luck that I was born in Germany. (If I / **be born** / in Britain / I / **visit** / Liverpool many times already)

5 I know I'll probably never go. (But if I / suddenly / **have** / the opportunity / I / **visit** / the houses in which John and Paul grew up) Well, one day maybe ...

Wiederholung: Die -*ing*-Form (*Gerund*) SB p. 200

Als *gerund* bezeichnet man die -*ing*-Form, wenn sie als **Nomen** verwendet wird.

gerund als **Subjekt**: **Swimming** is fun. *gerund* als **Objekt**: I love **swimming**.

Die -*ing*-Form folgt auf:

- bestimmte Verben, z. B. *imagine, dislike, miss, don't mind, enjoy*
- Präpositionen: I look forward to **seeing** you.

10 Cosplaying

Mohammed writes a post about games. Complete his post with the verbs from the box. Use the -*ing*-form. Tip: The prepositions after some of the gaps can help you find the right verb.

act • be • cosplay • learn • go • wear • take

I'm really interested in games and in ______________ about new trends. So I'm really looking forward to ______________ to the Bristol Anime and Gaming Con this year! Imagine ______________ among twenty thousand people who aren't frightened of ______________ part in new games, like cosplay, for example. Oh, have you never heard of cosplay? ______________ means ______________ the costume of a character in a game or film, for example, and ______________ the character.

-*ing*-Form (*Gerund*) oder *to* + Infinitiv (1) SB pp. 129, 201

Nach bestimmten Verben folgt:

- die *ing*-Form: *dislike, enjoy, finish, miss, imagine, practise, don't mind*
- *to*-Infinitiv: *want to, would like to, need to, decide to, hope to*
- -*ing*-Form **oder** *to*-Infinitiv: *prefer, hate, start, begin, like, love, continue*

More challenge 1 My first cosplay meeting

Mohammed writes about going to his first cosplay meeting. Circle the correct form of the verbs: -*ing*-form, *to* + infinitive, or both.

I started making / to make my costume months before my first cosplay meeting. This was really exciting, and I was proud of my costume when I had finished making / to make it! I practised acting / to act my character, and I found that my costume made me feel confident. I really enjoyed meeting / to meet lots of people who didn't mind wearing / to wear costumes. So I've decided going / to go to cosplay meetings again.

-*ing*-Form (*Gerund*) oder *to* + Infinitiv (2) SB pp. 129, 201

Diese Verben haben **unterschiedliche Bedeutungen**, je nachdem, ob sie mit *gerund* oder mit *to*-Infinitiv verwendet werden:

stop + *gerund*: I **stopped working** in the garden centre. ▶ mit etwas aufhören (es zu tun)

stop + *to* ...: I **stopped to have** a drink. ▶ aufhören, um etwas anderes zu tun

forget + *gerund*: I'll never **forget dancing** with you. ▶ vergessen, was man (früher) gemacht hat

forget + *to* ...: Oh! I **forgot to dance** with you! ▶ vergessen, was (noch) zu tun ist

remember + *gerund*: I **remember buying** my first phone. ▶ sich erinnern, was man mal getan hat

remember + *to* ...: I must **remember to send** this letter. ▶ daran denken, etwas (noch) zu tun

More challenge 2 E-sports at college

Read this text about studying e-sports at college. Then write the correct form of the verb in brackets: -*ing*-form or *to* + infinitive.

"I remember ________________ (take) part in my very first e-sports event," says Fatima Latif, who is now in her third year of studying e-sports at Dagenham College. "I was nervous about ________________ (make) mistakes! Now I feel great every time I finish ________________ (play)."

More and more young people want ________________ (study) e-sports. "But it's more than only about ________________ (play)," warns course leader Aarav Chakrabarti. "Our students have to organize e-sports events and must remember ________________ (think) of even the smallest detail. And students mustn't forget ________________ (stay) up-to-date with the latest changes in the gaming industry."

And what would Fatima like ________________ (do) after ________________ (leave) college? "I dream of ________________ (work) in the games industry," she says. Her chances are good. Spending on computer games is higher than on film, TV and music. Across the world, more than 200 million people stop whatever they're doing ________________ (watch) e-sports events. And that number is growing every year.

1 The Blue Mountains of Australia

Complete the text about a holiday in Australia using the right form of the verbs in brackets. There is one example (0) at the beginning.

> Lücken 1-4: Hier geht es um die Zeitformen. Achte auf Singalwörter: *last, before, since.* Sätze 5-6: Sieh dir die Struktur der Teilsätze genau an: *if ...*

On my last holiday in Australia, I *visited* ______________ (0 visit) the Blue Mountains. I ______________ (1 never hear) of them before, even though they ______________ (2 be) on the list of the UNESCO Heritage Site since the year 2000. I ______________ (3 go) on a hiking trip there and ______________ (4 have) a great view of the rock formation called the Three Sisters. They are spectacular and if I had to choose one favourite area, I ______________ (5 pick) this one. If I had had more time, I ______________ (6 love) to spend more days in the Blue Mountains.

2 A kayak tour in Syndey harbour

Read the advert. Sentences 1-5: Complete the sentences using adjective or adverb. You may need to use the comparative or superlative. Sentences 6-7: Complete the sentences using infinitive or the *ing*-form. Use the words in capitals at the end of each line to help you.

> Ein Adjektiv bezieht sich auf ein Nomen, ein Adverb auf ein Verb. Einsilbige und zweisilbige Adjektive auf *-y* steigerst du so: *nice – nicer – the nicest* Zweisilbige Adjektive, die nicht auf *-y* enden, oder mehrsilbige Adjektive werden mit *more/most* gesteigert.

0 Join us on an *unforgettable* ______________ tour of Sydney harbour! **FORGET**

1 Sydney harbour is one of the ______________ harbours in the world. **BEAUTY**

2 All our kayaks are safe, stable and ______________. **COMFORT**

3 You'll learn to use the kayak very ______________. **EASY**

4 Our trips are ______________ than the trips offered by most other companies. **GOOD**

5 We look forward to ______________ you! **WELCOME**

6 We are sure that you will want ______________ back again and again. **COME**

3 Peer pressure

Read this example of peer pressure. Complete the text with the right words in brackets.

Einige der Sätze stehen in der wörtlichen Rede. Achte auf die Zeitform im Einleitungssatz und denke an die Verschiebung der Zeitform in der Vergangenheit (S. 10).

Two weeks ago I (0) *found* ______ (found / find) out that my friends went shoplifting. I was shocked. You see, I (1) ______ (didn't do / hadn't done) anything like that before. But my friends laughed at me for (2) ______ (be / being) scared, and told me I (3) ______ (was / were) stupid. I (4) ______ (wanted / didn't want) to lose my friends, so last week I went into a shop with them and (5) ______ (steal / stole / have stolen) a scarf. But the following day the police came to my house and said they (6) ______ (have seen / had seen) me on CCTV. It was terrible. I (7) ______ (feel / feeling / felt) I had lost my parents' respect, and I promised that I (8) ______ (will / would) never steal again.

4 Respect

Read the sentences. There is a mistake in word order on ONE of the underlined parts in each sentence. (Circle) the part with the mistake. There is an example at the beginning (0).

0 Seretse Khama, <u>who was</u> the son of <u>an African king</u>, <u>was studying</u> (<u>in 1947 in London</u>).

1 <u>In 1948 married Seretse</u> a white English woman just one year after <u>he had first met her</u>.

2 <u>After the wedding</u> Ruth's father <u>refused to speak with her</u> because <u>she a black man had married</u>.

3 And the people in <u>Seretse's country</u>, <u>called Botswana</u>, <u>didn't accept</u> Ruth when she <u>there arrived</u>.

4 British people <u>wouldn't accept</u> a black queen, <u>so why they should accept</u> Ruth, <u>they asked angrily</u>.

5 But <u>Ruth showed respect for them</u> and soon <u>respected they</u> her and ignored her <u>skin colour</u>.

6 <u>Amazingly this is</u> a <u>true story that can you</u> see in <u>a film called</u> *United Kingdom*.

5 Applying for a job

Aisha lives and goes to school in York. Today she is applying for a holiday job. Complete the sentences.

- Put the words in *italics* in the right order.
- Write the correct form of the verbs in brackets.

There is an example at the beginning.

0 Aisha Khan, who lives in York, *a job / (apply for) / today*

Aisha Khan, who lives in York, is applying for a job today.

1 Aisha is still at school. She *(be) / since 2019 / at Haxby School*

Aisha is still at school. She ______________________________

2 Before she began at Haxby School, *(go) / Aisha / in York / to Primary School*

Before she began at Haxby School, ______________________________

3 Aisha *Primary School / (begin) / in 2014*

Aisha ______________________________

4 She *(be) / interested in / fit / (keep)*

She ______________________________

5 Aisha had experience of cleaning *when / she / for a cleaning company / (work)*

Aisha had experience of cleaning ______________________________

6 Unfortunately, *(not get) / Aisha / the job*

Unfortunately, ______________________________

7 If she *the job / (get), she (be) / very happy*

If she ______________________________

1 Life down under

Aufgabe 1

Wiederholung: Das *simple present* und das *present progressive* SB pp. 182/183

Du verwendest das *simple present* für alles, was **regelmäßig** stattfindet (wie Gewohnheiten oder Hobbys) und für alles, was **immer** so ist. Du benutzt oft die Wörter *always, never, often, sometimes, usually, on Fridays* mit dem *simple present.*

On Sundays, Mum **visits** Grandma and I **go** with her. Dad **doesn't come**.

Du verwendest das *present progressive* für alles, was **gerade im Gang** (noch nicht abgeschlossen) ist oder um ein **Bild zu beschreiben**. Du benutzt oft die Wörter *at the moment, now, today* mit dem *present progressive.*

What **are** you **doing** at the moment? – I **'m making** a paper plane.

! He isn't going. They aren't going. Aber: I'm not going.

Aufgaben 2 bis 4

Wiederholung: Das *going to-future* und das *will-future* SB p. 187

Das Futur mit ***going to*** wird verwendet,

- um über Vorhaben und Pläne für die Zukunft zu sprechen:

  What **are** you **going to** do at the weekend? – I **'m going to** go hiking with my dad.

- um auszudrücken, dass etwas gleich geschehen wird, weil es bereits Anzeichen dafür gibt:

  Look at those black clouds. It**'s going to** rain!

Das Futur mit ***will*** wird verwendet, um über die Zukunft zu sprechen. Es geht oft um

- Vermutungen oder Vorhersagen: I'm sure you **'ll feel** better tomorrow.
- Dinge, die wir nicht beeinflussen können:

  Will Christmas **be** on a Thursday next year?

- Spontane Hilfsangebote oder Versprechen:

  You don't look well. Do you know what? I **won't go** to the party. I **'ll stay** here with you.

Aufgaben 5 bis 6

Wiederholung: Das *simple past* und das *present perfect* SB *pp. 183, 185*

Mit dem *simple past* sagst du, wann etwas in der Vergangenheit passiert ist:

I **went** there last year.

Mit dem *present perfect* drückst du aus, dass etwas in der Vergangenheit geschehen ist – der genaue Zeitpunkt ist dabei unwichtig oder nicht bekannt. Oft haben die Handlungen auch Auswirkungen auf die Gegenwart:

Have you ever **been** to Sydney? – **I've been** there three times.

Aufgaben 7 bis 9

Wiederholung: Das *past perfect* SB *p. 186*

Mit dem *past perfect* drückst du aus, dass eine Handlung **vor einer anderen Handlung** oder **vor einem bestimmten Zeitpunkt in der Vergangenheit** stattfand. Das *past perfect* steht daher meist in einem Nebensatz; im zugehörigen Hauptsatz wird das *simple past* benutzt:

After the film **had ended**, I made a sandwich because I **hadn't eaten** any dinner.

2 Respect

Aufgaben 1 bis 3

Wiederholung: Die indirekte Rede *(Indirect speech)*: Aussagen SB *pp. 40, 192/193*

Wenn wir wörtlich wiedergeben, was jemand gesagt hat, verwenden wir die **direkte Rede** mit Anführungszeichen: Ruby said "I like you."

Wenn wir berichten, was jemand sagt, schreibt oder denkt, verwenden wir die **indirekte Rede** (ohne Anführungszeichen): Ruby told me (that) she liked me.

Veränderung der Zeitformen *(backshift of tenses)*: Ist das einleitende Verb *(told)* im *simple past*, wird in der indirekten Rede *simple present (like)* zu *simple past (liked).*

Neben den Verben werden häufig auch **Pronomen** (*me, her, them* usw.) und **Possessivbegleiter** (*my, her, their* usw.) verändert.

Die **Wortstellung** ist Subjekt – Verb – ... Das Wort *that* („dass") wird oft weggelassen.

Aufgabe 4

Indirekte Rede *(Indirect speech)*: Fragen (1) SB *pp. 41, 193*

Auch bei indirekten Fragen erfolgt der *backshift of tenses*, wenn das einleitende Verb im ***simple past*** steht *(asked, wanted to know)*.

Die Wortstellung in indirekten Fragen ist wie in Aussagesätzen: Subjekt - Verb -... Ist die direkte Frage eine Frage **ohne Fragewort** *(yes-no question)*, dann wird die indirekte Frage mit *if* oder *whether* (Deutsch: „ob") eingeleitet (ohne Komma):

„Do you buy lots of things online?" Sam asked his friend Amy.	Sam wanted to know **if** Amy bought lots of things online.
„Amina, did you watch the film last night?" I wanted to know.	I wanted to know **whether** Amina had watched the film the night before.

Wenn die direkte Frage **mit einem Fragewort** (*where? when? how?* usw.) beginnt, dann bleibt das Fragewort in der indirekten Frage erhalten:

„**Where** did you buy your hat?" Mum asked.	Mum asked **where** I had bought my hat.

Aufgabe 5

Die indirekte Rede (*Indirect speech*): Fragen (2) SB *pp. 41, 193*

Bei indirekten Fragen steht wie in der direkten Frage eine Präposition am Satzende:

"What job did Dan apply for?" Ari asked.	„Um welche Stelle hat Dan sich beworben?", fragte Ari.
Ari asked what job Dan had applied **for**.	Ari fragte, um welche Stelle Dan sich beworben habe.

Aufgaben 6 bis 7

Die indirekte Rede (*Indirect speech*): Aufforderungen, Bitten, Ratschläge SB *pp. 41, 194*

Bitten, Aufforderungen und Ratschläge werden in der Regel mit der **Infinitiv-Form** wiedergegeben:
Bei **Auffordnungen: *tell*** *somebody* ***to do*** *something*:

"Don't do that!" my friend said.	→ My friend told me not to do that.

Bei **Bitten**: ***ask*** *somebody* ***to do*** *something*:

"Please pass me the jam," my sister said.	→ My sister asked me to pass her the jam.

Bei **Ratschlägen: *advise*** *somebody* ***to do*** *something*:

"I don't think you should go there," he said.	→ He advised me not to go there.

Aufgabe 8

Wiederholung: Die indirekte Rede: Verschiebung der Zeitformen

SB *pp. 42, 193/194*

Steht das einleitende Verb in der Vergangenheit, werden die Zeitformen der direkten Rede meist um eine Zeitstufe in die Vergangenheit „zurückverschoben" *(backshift of tenses)*.

	Direkte Rede	Indirekte Rede: *Nav said (that) ...*
present progressive → past progressive	"I'**m** playing a new game."	he **was** playing a new game.
simple present → simple past	"I **check** my phone every day."	he **checked** his phone every day.
simple past → past perfect	"I **posted** photos of myself."	he **had** posted photos of himself.
present perfect → past perfect	"I **have** never tried a digital detox."	he **had** never tried a digital detox.
will → would *can → could*	"I **will** upload the film when I **can**."	he **would** upload the film when he **could**.
am/are/is going to → was/were going to	"I **am** not going to shut my account."	he **was** not going to shut his account.

Aufgaben More challenge 1 More challenge 2

Partizipialkonstruktionen

SB *pp. 52, 199*

Partizipialkonstruktionen verwendet man vor allem im geschriebenen Englisch. Sie stehen **anstelle von Nebensätzen** und geben Informationen über die **Zeit**, den **Grund** oder die **Begleitumstände** einer Handlung.

Du verwendest in diesen Partizipialkonstruktionen das **Partizip Präsens** (present participle). Du kennst es schon von den Verlaufsformen.

Du bildest es so: Verb + *-ing*

While **running** down the street, I saw something strange.	= wann? (*While I was running down the street ...*)
Feeling ill, he decided to stay in bed.	= warum? (*Because he felt ill ...*)
William built a windmill **using** a bike.	= wie? (*William used a bike to build ...*)

Steht die Partizipialkonstruktion **vor** dem Hauptsatz, kannst du die Konjunktion weglassen.

I saw something strange while **running** down the street.

Running down the street, I saw something strange.

3 Looking forward

Aufgabe 1

Wortstellung in Aussagen (1) SB *pp. 66, 188*

In Aussagesätzen gilt immer die Regel ***subject – verb – object*** (S-V-O).

	Subjekt	Verb	Objekt		Subjekt	Verb	
	I	play	tennis.				
Yesterday	I	didn't play	tennis	because	I	was	too tired.

Adverbien der Zeit und Häufigkeit (*already, just, never, often*) stehen **vor** einem *past participle*.

I have **never** played tennis.

Die Adverbien, die dem ganzen Satz den Ton geben (*luckily, unfortunately*) stehen meist am **Satzanfang**.

Unfortunately, I can't play the guitar.

Adverbien, die sich auf ein Verb bzw. eine Tätigkeit beziehen, stehen meist am Satzende.

After her date with Ben, Lia walked home **happily**.

Aufgaben 2 bis 3

Wortstellung in Aussagen (2) SB *pp. 66, 188*

Gibt es in einem Satz eine Orts- und eine Zeitangabe, gilt die Regel: **Ort** vor **Zeit**.

Ben met Li **at the youth club** **three weeks ago**.

Aufgaben 4 bis 7

Wortstellung in Fragesätzen

SB pp. 66, 189

In Fragesätzen verwendet man das Hilfsverb *do/does* im *simple present* und *did* im *simple past*. Das Vollverb steht im Infinitiv (*feel, play, swim*). Bei der 3. Person Singular braucht das Vollverb kein *-s*, denn es steckt schon in *does*.

In Fragesätzen steht das Hilfsverb vor dem Subjekt. Das Vollverb steht – wie im Aussagesatz – nach dem Subjekt. Fragewörter stehen – wie im Deutschen – am Anfang des Satzes.

Fragewort	Hilfsverb	Subjekt	Vollverb	Objekt	
	Does	your friend	start	a new job	tomorrow?
Where	do	you	start	your new job?	

In Fragen mit *be* wird das Hilfsverb *do* **nicht** verwendet. **Is** your friend reliable?

Aufgabe 8

Fragen im Passiv

SB pp. 125, 190

Fragen im Passiv bildest du mit ***be + past participle***:

Fragewort	*be*	Subjekt	*Past Participle*	
	Was	James	**hurt**	in the accident?
Where	**was**	he	**hurt**?	

Aufgabe 9 bis 10

Fragen mit Modalverben

SB pp. 125, 190

Ja/Nein-Fragen mit *modals* beginnen mit dem Modalverb Das Hilfsverb *do* wird **nicht** verwendet.

Brauchst du auch ein Fragewort, steht dieses noch vor dem Modalverb.

Fragewort	Modalverb	Subjekt	Vollverb	
	May	I	go out	this evening, Dad?
What time	**must**	I	come	home?

Aufgaben **More challenge 1** **More challenge 2**

Subjekt- und Objektfragen

SB *pp. 125, 189*

a) Fragen nach dem Subjekt

Fragt man nach dem Subjekt eines Aussagesatzes, (Frage: „Wer oder was?"), braucht man kein Hilfsverb, da das Fragewort das Subjekt ersetzt. Dies ist sehr häufig bei den Fragewörtern *who, which* und *what* der Fall. Die Wortstellung ist wie im Aussagesatz:

Fragewort (= Subjekt)	Vollverb	
Who	was	the first man on the moon?
(Neil Armstrong	*was*	*the first man on the moon.)*
What	has	eight legs and scares people?
(Spiders	*have*	*eight legs and scare people.)*

Das ist im Deutschen genauso.

b) Fragen nach dem Objekt

Fragen nach dem Objekt eines Aussagesatzes bildet man mit einem Hilfsverb, z.B. *do/does/did.*

Fragewort (= Objekt)	Hilfsverb	Subjekt	Vollverb	
Who	did	you	see	yesterday?
(You saw a famous person yesterday)				
What	does	she	like?	
(She likes music.)				

Aufgaben **More challenge 3** **More challenge 4** **More challenge 5** **More challenge 6**

Fragen mit Fragewörtern und Präpositionen

SB *pp. 126, 190*

Präpositionen stehen vor Nomen (***after** lunch, **with** my friends*) und kommen oft in Wendungen mit Verben vor (*look **at**, wait **for**, fit **in with***).

Wenn du **Fragen mit Präpositionen** bildest, stehen

- die **Fragewörter** am **Anfang** der Frage.
- die **Präpositionen** am **Ende** der Frage.

Vorsicht: das ist anders als im Deutschen, wo die Präpositionen meist vor dem Fragewort stehen oder ein neues Fragewort mit *wo-* beginnt.

Fragewort		Präposition	
Who	did he walk	**with**?	(Mit wem ging er spazieren?)
Which	team do you play	**for**?	(Für welche Mannschaft spielst du?)
What	are you looking	**forward to**?	(Worauf freust du dich?)

Aufgaben 11 bis 13

Frageanhängsel (*Question tags*) SB *pp. 67, 203*

Question tags werden im Englischen **in Gesprächen** verwendet. Man benutzt sie,

- um **Zustimmung** zu erreichen.
- als echte **Nachfrage**, wenn man unsicher ist.

Die englischen *question tags* entsprechen gell?/oder?/nicht wahr?/ne? im Deutschen.

Bildung der Frageanhängsel

Die *question tags* richten sich nach dem **Verb** und nach der **Person** im Satz.

- Bei *be* und Modalverben wird das Verb verneint (ein negatives Verb wird bejaht).
- Bei Vollverben (*play, work, eat*) wird die Verneinung durch *don't/doesn't* bzw. *didn't* gezeigt, die Bejahung durch *do/does* bzw. *did*
- Die Person bleibt gleich. Personennamen (Jack, Sara) werden durch Pronomen (*he, she*) ersetzt.

Bejahter Satz + verneintes Frageanhängsel	Verneinter Satz + bejahtes Frageanhängsel
Noah **is** angry, **isn't** he?	You **aren't** going to leave, **are** you?
It**'s** raining, **isn't** it?	Ellie **isn't** ill, **is** she?
There **is** a cat in the garden, **isn't** there?	I **won't** finish my work in time, **will** I?
We **can** win, **can't** we?	We **mustn't** go there, **must** we?
They **live** in Manchester, **don't** they?	You **don't work** here, **do** you?

4 Generation *like*

Aufgabe 1

Wiederholung: Bedingungssätze, Typ 1 (1) SB *p. 196*

Mit Bedingungssätzen vom Typ 1 drückst du aus, was unter bestimmten Bedingungen passieren kann oder passieren wird. Sie bestehen aus zwei Teilsätzen: Die Bedingung steht im *if*-Satz (Nebensatz). Das Verb steht hier im *simple present*. Der Hauptsatz beschreibt, was folgt, wenn die Bedingung erfüllt wird. Das Verb steht meist im *will-future*.

if-Nebensatz (Bedingung):	Hauptsatz (Folge):
simple present	***will-future***
If they **come** early,	I**'ll be** surprised.

Der *if*-Satz kann vor oder nach dem Hauptsatz stehen. Anders als im Deutschen setzt man **kein** Komma, wenn der *if*-Satz am Ende steht.

We won't be in trouble if they don't see us.

Aufgabe 2

Wiederholung: Bedingungssätze, Typ 1 (2) SB p. 196

In Bedingungssätzen können im **Hauptsatz** statt *will-future* auch stehen:

- **Modalverb (*can/must/should*):**

If you need help, you **can/must/should** call me.

- **Imperativ:**

If you need help, **call** me.

Aufgaben 3 bis 4

Wiederholung: Bedingungssätze, Typ 2 SB p. 197

Bedingungssätze vom Typ 2 beschreiben, was unter bestimmten Bedingungen passieren würde. „Was wäre, wenn ..." Der Nebensatz mit *if* beschreibt oft eine **unwahrscheinliche oder unsichere Bedingung**. Im Hauptsatz steht, was in diesem Fall passieren würde. Im Deutschen verwendet man hier oft würde/wäre/hätte.

if-Nebensatz:	Hauptsatz:
simple past	***would/wouldn't / could/couldn't / might (not)***
If my parents **gave** me some money,	I **would buy** a new phone.
If I **had** an older phone,	I **couldn't watch** films on it.
If I **didn't have** a phone,	I **might go** mad.

Aufgaben 5 bis 9

Bedingungssätze, Typ 3 SB pp. 89, 197

Mit *If*-Sätzen Typ 3 stellst du dir vor, was in der Vergangenheit unter bestimmten Bedingungen hätte geschehen können: „Was wäre gewesen, wenn ..."

if-Nebensatz:	*Hauptsatz:*
past perfect	***would/wouldn't have / could/couldn't have / might (not) have + past participle***
If my parents **had given** me some money,	I **would have bought** a new phone.
If I **had been** more careful,	I **might not have read** that new message.
If we **had shared** the information,	we **could have gone** to the concert together.

Die Kurzform sowohl von ***had*** als auch von ***would*** ist ***'d***.

If they'**d** stayed at home, they'**d** have missed a good film at the cinema.

Aufgabe 10

Wiederholung: Die *-ing*-Form (*Gerund*) SB *p. 200*

Als *gerund* bezeichnet man die *-ing*-Form, wenn sie als **Nomen** verwendet wird.

gerund als **Subjekt**: **Swimming** is fun.

gerund als **Objekt**: I love **swimming**.

Die *-ing*-Form folgt auf:

- bestimmte Verben, z. B. *imagine, dislike, miss, don't mind, enjoy*
- Präpositionen: I look forward to **seeing** you.

Aufgabe More challenge 1

***-ing*-Form (*Gerund*) oder *to* + Infinitiv (1)** SB *pp. 129, 201*

Nach bestimmten Verben folgt:

- die *ing*-Form: *dislike, enjoy, finish, miss, imagine, practise, don't mind*
- *to*-Infinitiv: *want to, would like to, need to, decide to, hope to*
- *-ing*-Form **oder** *to*-Infinitiv: *prefer, hate, start, begin, like, love, continue*

Aufgabe More challenge 2

***-ing*-Form (*Gerund*) oder *to* + Infinitiv (2)** SB *pp. 129, 201*

Diese Verben haben **unterschiedliche Bedeutungen**, je nachdem, ob sie mit *gerund* oder mit *to*-Infinitiv verwendet werden:

stop + *gerund*: I **stopped working** in the garden centre. ▶ mit etwas aufhören (es zu tun)

stop + *to* ...: I **stopped to have** a drink. ▶ aufhören, um etwas anderes zu tun

forget + *gerund*: I'll never **forget dancing** with you. ▶ vergessen, was man (früher) gemacht hat

forget + *to* ...: Oh! I **forgot to dance** with you! ▶ vergessen, was (noch) zu tun ist

remember + *gerund*: I **remember buying** my first phone. ▶ sich erinnern, was man mal getan hat

remember + *to* ...: I must **remember to send** this letter. ▶ daran denken, etwas (noch) zu tun

1 Life down under

1 An interview on the beach

Tara: This afternoon, I**'m visiting** the beach. Most people here **are having** fun, but Mel is different. She **isn't just playing** in the sand. Actually, she **comes** here often. What **are you doing** here today, Mel?

Mel: I**'m not playing**. – I**'m training**! I **come** here most days to train.

Tara: What sport **do you play** when you come here.

Mel: I **play** beach volleyball. My partner Ali is over there, look – she**'s running** along the beach.

Tara: How often **do you practise**?

Mel: We **practise** for hours every day, but we **don't train** outside if it's too wet – we **go** to the gym. At the moment, we **are preparing** for the next Olympics.

2 Saying goodbye

Mia: Do you know what? We**'re going to move** to South Australia in summer.

Miro: To South Australia? Why **are you going to do** that?

Mia: Because my dad has a new job. He**'s going to help** to build a new wind farm.

Miro: Oh! And where **are you going to go** to school?

Mia: I don't know yet. Dad says, he**'s going to ask** some of his colleagues about schools there.

Miro: Oh dear, I**'m going to miss** you, Mia.

Mia: Me too, Miro. But we can keep in contact. We**'re going to video-chat** every week. And you**'re going to visit** me in the holidays.

Miro: Yes, let's do that!

3 A new wind farm in South Australia

To achieve its goal of using only renewable energy by 2030, Australia has a number of onshore wind farms. When it is finished, Carmody's Hill wind farm in South Australia **will** be one of four wind farms in that area. Building the wind farm **will** take 18 months. How much electricity **will** the new field make? We **won't** know the answer till we know how big the new wind turbines **will** be. 8.5% of Australia's electricity came from wind farms in 2019 and it is hoped that this **will** continue to go up. The result, of course, is that, in the future, Australia **won't** need as much coal and gas as it does now.

4 Snow!

1 **Are you going to** go skiing?
2 No, they said on TV that there **won't** be enough snow.
3 It looks like **I'm going to** have a problem.
4 I **will** help you.
5 Then I **will** go skiing after all!

5 In the summer holidays

1 What did **you do in the holidays?**
2 **Did you have a good time?**
3 **Who did you go with?**
4 **Did you visit Uluru?**
5 **Did you bring me a present?**

6 Feelings

1 Miro is tired. He **has cleaned** the kitchen and the bathroom.
2 Lisa and Ray are excited. They **have never been** to a live concert.
3 I'm scared: our neighbours **have bought** a really big dog.
4 Mr Robert is angry because someone **has broken** his window.
5 Zonia feels nervous because she **hasn't worked** hard enough for the test.
6 Koen feels lonely. He **hasn't talked** to anyone all afternoon.

7 Not a good day for Kylie

	first	after that
2	a	b
3	a	b
4	b	a
5	b	a

8 Visiting Aunt Jane

			1							
			F							
	2	B	O	U	G	H	T			3
			R							M
			G					5		A
4	C	O	O	K	E	D		F		D
			T			6	D	O	N	E
7	P	U	T					U		
			E					N		
	8	I	N	V	I	T	E	D		

9 An interview

Tara: Today **I'm talking** to Krish. He **owns** a gym here in Sydney. **How many members does your gym have**, Krish?

Krish: My gym **has** about 3,000 members, although most members **don't come** regularly. For example, lots of people **joined** the gym last January – maybe because friends **had given** them a membership for Christmas. Most of those new members **came** only once or twice in January and then they **stopped**. Perhaps they **hadn't really wanted** a membership. About 600 of our members **use** the gym almost every week. At the moment, ten people **are doing** Zumba over there. The teacher **teaches** yoga every week too.

Tara: **When did you open** the gym, Krish?

Krish: I opened the gym when I **moved** to Australia 18 years ago. When I **grew up** in India, I often **dreamed** of living here.

Tara: **Did you train** a lot when you lived in India?

Krish: I **didn't train** at a gym. But one day, I **saw** people at a gym on TV. I **thought**: "I **want** to do that!" That TV programme **changed** my life!

2 Respect

1 A review

1 The review said that all the magazines really **liked** this new game.
2 It said that the game **took** ideas from other games and **used** them in new ways.
3 The writer of the review thought that the graphics **were** awesome.
4 And the writer claimed that players **experienced** a lot of action.
5 The review warned that it **could be** hard to play if you **didn't play** games often.
6 But to sum up, the writer's opinion was that it **was** worth buying this game because it **gave** you a good time.

2 Hide-and-seek

1 First Diya told me that she could see **me**.
2 Then she told Emily that she could see **her**.
3 She told Jon and Kiera that she could see **them**.
4 Last of all she told Harry that she could see **him**.

3 Respect in the digital world

a)
1 She said **she was** an influencer and **(that) she promoted** products that **she** really **liked**.
2 She added that in **her** opinion as an influencer **she had to** respect **her** followers.
3 She said **she** always **told** them when **she was** paid to talk about something.

b)
1 "**I use** a digitally controlled wheelchair, but that **isn't my biggest problem**."
2 **"My real problem is that people often talk to me very slowly as if I'm / I was / I were stupid or deaf."**
3 **"When I go out with my sister, people don't talk to me directly but ask my sister how I am / I'm feeling."**

4 A job interview

a)
1 The man asked whether Natalie **was OK** and if she **needed an ambulance**.
2 He asked **if/whether she/Natalie had broken her leg**.
3 He wanted to know **if/whether she would be able to walk**.

b)
1 "What sort of graphics **do you like best**?"
2 "Where **have you learned / did you learn computer programming**?"
3 "When **will you be able to start**?"
4 **"How much did you earn in your last job?"**

5 Zendaya and her mum

2 My mum asked me **who I had been talking to**.
3 She asked me **what I was checking my phone for**.
4 She asked me **what I was worried about**.
5 And she asked me **what I had uploaded photos of**.
6 Then she asked me **what I had written about**.
7 And then she asked me **which social media platforms I was on**.
8 And then my mum asked me **who I now go out with**.
9 She asked me **what I was thinking of** – a person like that!

6 Good advice?

1 Amy advised me **to talk** about my interests.
2 Carl advised me **not to panic** and **to stay** calm.
3 Max advised me **not to worry** too much about my clothes and **to wear** something comfortable.
4 Cindy advised me **to do** something active and **not to meet** in a café.

7 Tim's evening

1 Sam messaged me and **asked/told** me **to meet** him in the New World Café.
2 I told him I'd rather go for a walk and **told/asked** him **to come** to the park instead.
3 Sam was dressed very smartly while I was wearing jeans and sneakers. I told him you had **advised** me **to wear** something comfortable. He laughed.

8 A survey about social media

1 Mohammed said that **he didn't need** social media to keep in touch with **his** friends.
2 Lukas said in **his** opinion, social media **had saved** lives after many accidents.
3 Hannah said **(that) she hoped** social media **would help her** to make new friends.
4 Sophia said **(that) she had begun** to use social media at primary school.
5 Felix **was** sure social media **were going** to influence our lives more and more.
6 Radhia **thought (that)** social media platforms **were getting** better.

More challenge 1 Strange ways

* **Wearing** his shoes on his hands, writer William Faulkner wrote his books with his feet.
* Ludwig van Beethoven often wrote music while **having** a bath.
* **Wanting** to finish his books on time, writer Victor Hugo did not leave his house until he was finished – even though they were often over 1,000 pages long!
* Inventor Nikola Tesla said that he was in love with a bird that he found, **taking** it home to live with him.
* Bill Gates programmes and has meetings while **sitting** in a special chair that moves.
* Inventor Dr Yoshiro Nakamatsu thought of ideas for inventions while **swimming** underwater.
* **Being** afraid of illness, actress Cameron Diaz opens doors with her elbows.

More challenge 2 A strange dream

a)
2 **(While) standing on two legs, the deer smiled at me and said hello.**
3 **Being polite, I said hello back even though I was confused.**
4 **Then I saw a bird flying through the forest and singing my favourite song.**
5 **(When) running towards the bird, I fell over.**
6 **Falling to the floor, I called the deer to help me.**

b)
1 **Wanting to talk to me, my teacher suddenly arrived.**
2 **Hearing that I hadn't done my homework, she looked angry.**
3 **(When) getting up, I found a Christmas present.**
4 **(When) giving the present to my teacher, I told her that it was my homework.**
5 **Taking the present from me, she smiled.**

3 Looking forward

1 You are the teacher

1 In the photo I **can** see a tent.
2 Two people have **already** started cooking.
3 Unfortunately, it **has** just started to rain.
4 We **always** stay in a hotel when we go away.
5 So I have **never** been camping.
6 But of course I think it could **be** fun.

2 A festival of world music

1 I heard a South African band at a concert **in Berlin two years ago**.
2 And I went to this festival **here in Berlin two months later / a few months later**.
3 Now I come **here every year**.
4 I heard a great band from Cape Town **here on Friday**.
5 Now I'd like to travel **to South Africa next year**.

3 A new job

1 I was happy **when I got my part-time job.**
2 On the first day **I walked there nervously.**
3 I got to know **my colleagues very quickly.**
4 Now we often **meet in a café after work.**

4 Questions at an interview

Employer: Good morning. Please sit down. I'm going to ask you a few questions. First of all, **how** old are you?
Candidate: I'm 17.
Employer: You said you had a part-time job. **Where** do you work?
Candidate: In the cake shop in Sheep Street.
Employer: And **how many** hours a week do you work there?
Candidate: Four hours on Saturday, and sometimes more in the holidays.
Employer: And **how much** do you earn per hour?
Candidate: The minimum wage.
Employer: And can you tell me please: **Why** do you want to change jobs?
Candidate: I'd like to earn a bit more money.

Employer: And **when** could you start working with us?
Candidate: I could start in two weeks.
Employer: That sound all right. Oh, **who** is your boss in the shop?
Candidate: Ms Reed.
Employer: I'll need to contact her of course ...

5 The Edinburgh Fringe Festival

b) + c)

1 When **did** the Edinburgh Fringe Festival put on its first show? – In **1947**.
2 In which month **does** the festival always take place? – In **August**.
3 **Do** you have to pay for the tickets? – **For some, not all**.
4 Over how many days **did** the festival take place in 2018? – **25 days**.
5 And how many shows **did** the festival put on in 2018? – **Over 3500**.
6 **Does** the Edinburgh Fringe Festival usually sell more tickets than the Olympic Games? – **No (, it doesn't).**
7 Where **do** the shows take place? – In many different **places.**
8 Why **did** no shows take place in 2020? – Because of the **(Covid) pandemic.**

6 Food: are you boring or brave?

a)

1 **Can you cook?**
2 **What do you usually order in a restaurant?**
3 **How many types of food do you hate?**
4 **Do you like to try the local food when you are on holiday? / When you are on holiday, do you like to try the local food?**

b) a4, b1, c3, d2

7 Messaging a friend

1 **Did you have a good trip back to Edinburgh?**
2 **Was your plane on time?**
3 **Which German food did you like best?**
4 **Did your cousin take you there?**
5 **Were you always able to understand us?**
6 **Do you want to come again next year?**

8 A quiz

a)

1 **Was** the Eiffel Tower built in 1789 or 1889? – **1889**
2 **Were** the Harry Potter books written by a man or a woman? – **a woman**
3 **Was** the book *Oliver Twist* written in 1838 or 1938? – **1838**
4 **Were** carrots brought to Europe from Turkey or America? – **(from) Turkey**

b)

1 When **was** penicillin **discovered**? – **1928**
2 Where **were** women first **given** the right to vote? – **New Zealand**
3 Where **was** the world's first football league **founded**? – **England**

c)

1 Which US city **is known** as the Big Apple? – **New York**
2 Which language **is spoken** by most people in the world? – **Chinese (as a first language) or English (as first and second language)**
3 Where **are** most films **made**? – **India**

9 Looking for a new flat

1 **Can I have pets?**
2 **Must I be quiet after 10 pm?**
3 **May I play my ukulele?**
4 **Should I take this flat?**

10 At the railway station

Woman: Good morning. **How can I help you?**
Hamza: I'd like a ticket for the 9.53 train to York, please. **When will it arrive in York?**
Woman: At 12.25.
Hamza: OK, thanks. **May I take my bike on the train?**
Woman: Yes, of course.
Hamza: And I'd like to have a coffee. **Where should I buy it?**
Woman: You can buy really nice coffee on the train.

More challenge 1 Noises in the night

Ben: I was scared last night.
Rosh: What **scared** you?
Ben: A loud noise.
Rosh: What **happened** then?
Ben: I switched on my phone. That worked.
Rosh: What do you mean? What **worked**?
Ben: I watched a good film. And I fell asleep. But then I heard a loud noise again!
Rosh: Oh no! What **was** it?
Ben: My alarm clock.

More challenge 2 A rap

a)

What **did** you think I was going to do?
What **were** you scared of?
What **will/would** it take to make you understand that I'm a New Yorker too?
What **would** it feel like, to know you'll never fit in?
What **would** your life be like in my skin?
What **do** you think when you look at me?
Tell me, what **do/can** you see?

Your mind is so narrow – what **can/could** I do to open it wider?
What **can/could** I say to show you I'm not an outsider?
Who **do** you think you are?
What **will** you say when I'm a star?

b)
1 Who **moved** away when Idris sat in the subway? – A **businessman**.
2 How **does** Idris feel that he is different? – He **doesn't look like the businessman.** / He **looks different.**
3 What **did** Idris say he will be later in life? – A **star**.

More challenge 3 Stopped by the police
1 What were you looking **at**?
2 What were you waiting **for**?
3 What were you frightened **of**?
4 Which restaurant had you eaten **in**?
5 When were you there **till**?
6 What were you talking **about**?
7 Who do you live **with**?
8 Which school do you go **to**?

More challenge 4 Questions to a new friend
1 **Which town do you live in?**
2 **Who do you live with?**
3 **What do you dream about?**

More challenge 5 Looking for a new job
1 Which school **do you go to**?
2 What sort of shop **do you work in**?
3 What sort of **job are you looking for**?
4 When **can you start from**?

More challenge 6 Mediation
1 **Where do you come from?**
2 **Who do you stay with?**
3 **Which nearby places have you been to?**
4 **Which hospital are you working in?**
5 **Which people do you look after?**
6 **What are you looking forward to when you are back in Australia?**

11 Thoughts in a club
1 That boy Alek is Polish, **isn't he?**
2 He doesn't live here, **does he?**
3 But he can dance well, **can't he?**
4 And he really likes dancing, **doesn't he?**
5 Well, I'm not shy, **am I?**
6 So I can ask him to dance with me, **can't I?**
7 Alek! Alek! Oh dear, the music is too loud! He can't hear me, **can he?**
8 I'll have to dance with Lawson after all, **won't I?**

12 In a new flat
a)
1 The flat is great, **isn't** it?
2 Our neighbours are nice, **aren't** they?
3 They brought some tea and biscuits. That was really kind, **wasn't** it?
4 The rooms aren't very big, **are** they?
5 There isn't any room for the wardrobe, **is** there?
6 But we're very happy here, **aren't** we?

b)
1 The big sofa looks good over here, **doesn't it?**
2 We only just got it through the front door, **didn't we?**
3 The curtains go well with the carpet, **don't they?**
4 The noise from the street doesn't matter, **does it?**
5 We didn't have any big problems, **did we?**
6 But we don't want to move again for a long time now, **do we?**

13 Rugby: a game with strange rules
1 There are fifteen players in a team, **aren't there?**
2 You use a ball that isn't round, **don't you?**
3 It isn't a summer sport, **is it?**
4 You can hold the ball in your hands, **can't you?**
5 But you can't pass the ball forwards, **can you?**
6 You don't score by kicking the ball into a goal, **do you?**
7 It's a popular sport in Wales, **isn't it?**
8 You must try to stop the other players, **mustn't you?**

4 Generation *like*

1 Have you heard this before?
1 If you **play** too many games, you **will get** addicted.
2 Your eyes **will get** worse if you **watch** the screen too long.
3 Your school work **will suffer** it you **use** your phone at school.
4 If you **use** your phone in bed, you **won't get** enough sleep.
5 If you **use** social media, people **will know** everything about you.
6 People **won't be able** to read books if they **watch** their screens all day.

2 Good advice for using social media

If you use social media, you should choose your friends carefully.
You musn't tell your friends if you have a secret.
If you are busy, you can answer your messages later.
Don't answer a message if you don't know who sent it.

3 Without my phone for a week

If I **didn't have** my phone for a week, I think I **wouldn't know** what to do! I think I **would feel** lonely if I **didn't chat** with my friends. And my homework **would be** harder if I **wasn't able to go** online. But on the other hand I **might spend** more time with my dog. And if we **went** for a long walk together, we **would have** good fun.

4 Not always what you think

If you **saw** me with my friends, you **would imagine** that I'm a confident teenager who loves sharing pictures of myself. Some of my friends **wouldn't care** if their photos **were shown** on the internet. But I **would hate** it if people **showed** pictures of me. I'm really shy!
If you **didn't know** me well, you **would guess** I'm a typical screenager. I bet you **wouldn't believe** me if I **told** you that I actually don't use my phone much. In fact, if you **want** to find me after school, **you'll see** me on a sports field – but definitely not on my phone!

5 If we had known …

a)
1C If I had known that children in poor countries make lots of our cheap jeans and T-shirts, I would have bought my clothes in different shops.
2D If we had thought more deeply about the damage that plastic does in the ocean, we would have bought fewer drinks in plastic bottles.
3A If I had known that so many people suffer from cyberbullying, I would have been more careful with the language I use in messages.
4E If I had known how much discrimination there is against people of colour, I would have tried harder to make friends with students from different backgrounds.
5B If I had known some of the horrible things that people can do online with photos, I would have shared fewer pictures of myself on social media.
6F If I had realized how exciting online games are, I would have learned to play more of them earlier.

b)
1 If I had known that there are so many dangerous materials in phones, **I would have kept my old phone longer.**
2 If I had known that flying causes so much air pollution, **I wouldn't have flown so often.**
3 If I had seen the amazing work that some charities do, **I would have given them more money.**

6 A special birthday activity

type 1:
If I have to get up early for something important, I won't hear my alarm.
I learned that if you go too fast, the surfboard will rise and you'll fall into the water.
… if Aqila asks me for a fun activity for her birthday, I'll have to think of something really good!
Or if I can't think of anything else, maybe we'll go jet surfing again!

type 2:
… if I had the choice of any activity on my birthday, I'd choose jet surfing.
… and if someone asked me for a tip for a birthday, I'd definitely recommend jet surfing.
So if we went again, I'd definitely book a longer time for the surfing.

type 3:
… and we would never have arrived at the jet surfing centre in time if Aqila's mum hadn't driven us there.
If our trainer hadn't helped me, I might never have been able to even to stand!
I'd happily have paid for a second hour if other people hadn't already booked it.

7 What if?

a)

If ...

If I **hadn't lost** my phone that day,
my life **would have been** so different.

My bus pass is on my phone,
so I **would have taken** the bus
if I **had had** my phone.

I **would have gone** by bike
If someone **hadn't stolen** it

I **would have asked** my dad
to drive me into town
If I **had had** the chance to phone him

But instead I walked, feeling
fed up because of the rain,
and thinking of all the calls I was missing

If I **had known**, I **wouldn't have minded**.

Because if I **hadn't walked**
You **wouldn't have seen** me on the street.

If the weather **had been** good
You **wouldn't have offered** to
share your umbrella.

If we **hadn't talked** for hours,
forgetting where we were,
We **wouldn't have fallen** in love

I'm so glad I lost my phone that day ...

b)

1 If Harry **hadn't walked**, he **wouldn't have met** his future partner.
2 If his future partner **had gone** a different way, they **would have missed** each other.
3 And they **wouldn't have spoken** to each other if Harry's future partner **hadn't brought** a big umbrella.

8 Lucky or unlucky?

b)

1 If it **hadn't been** foggy, Frank would have been able to see the path.
2 If Frank **hadn't shouted** for help, nobody would have seen him.
3 If a hiker **hadn't heard** him, Frank might have died of cold.

c)

4 If the hiker hadn't had a phone, he **couldn't/wouldn't have phoned** for help.
5 If the air ambulance service hadn't used jet suits, they **couldn't/wouldn't have reached** Frank so quickly.
6 If they had had to walk up the mountain, they **would have been** much slower.

d)

7 **If the helicopter hadn't come, Frank wouldn't/couldn't have got to the hospital so quickly.**
8 **If Frank hadn't gone to the Lake District that day, he wouldn't have fallen.**

9 A Beatles fan

1 **type 1: I will always be happy if I hear one of their songs.**
2 **type 3: If I had been a teenager in the 1960s, I might/could/would have seen the Beatles.**
3 **type 2: If I earned more money, I would book a flight to Liverpool at once.**
4 **type 3: If I had been born in Britain, I would have visited Liverpool many times already.**
5 **type 1: But if I suddenly have the opportunity, I will visit the houses in which John and Paul grew up.**

10 Cosplaying

I'm really interested in games and in **learning** about new trends. So I'm really looking forward to **going** to the Bristol Anime and Gaming Con this year! Imagine **being** among twenty thousand people who aren't frightened of **taking** part in new games, like cosplay, for example. Oh, have you never heard of cosplay? **Cosplaying** means **wearing** the costume of a character in a game or film, and **acting** the character.

More challenge 1 My first cosplay meeting

I started **making/to make** my costume months before my first cosplay meeting. This was really exciting, and I was proud of my costume when I had finished **making** it!

I practised **acting** my character, and I found that my costume made me feel confident. I really enjoyed **meeting** lots of other people who didn't mind **wearing** costumes.

So I've decided **to go** to cosplay meetings again.

More challenge 2 E-sports at college

"I remember **taking** part in my very first e-sports event," says Fatima Latif, who is now in her third year of studying e-sports at Dagenham College. "I was nervous about **making** mistakes! Now I feel great every time I finish **playing**."

More and more young people want **to study** e-sports. "But it's more than only about **playing**," warns course leader Aarav Chakrabarti. "Our students have to organize e-sports events and must remember **to think** of even the smallest detail. And students mustn't forget **to stay** up-to-date with the latest changes in the gaming industry."

And what would Fatima like **to do** after **leaving** college? "I dream of **working** in the games industry," she says. Her chances are good. Spending on computer games is higher than on film, TV and music. Across the world, more than 200 million people stop whatever they're doing **to watch** e-sports events. And that number is growing every year.

Exam file

1 The Blue Mountains of Australia

On my last holiday in Australia, I visited the Blue Mountains. I **had never heard** of them before, even though they **have been** on the list of the UNESCO Heritage Site since the year 2000.
I **went** on a hiking trip there and **had** a great view of a rock formation called the Three Sisters. They are spectacular and if I had to choose one favourite area, I **would pick** this one. If I had had more time, I **would have loved** to spend more days in the Blue Mountains.

2 A kayak tour in Sydney harbour

0 Join us on an unforgettable tour of Sydney harbour!
1 Sydney harbour is one of the **most beautiful** harbours in the world.
2 All our kayaks are safe, stable and **comfortable**.
3 You'll learn to use the kayak very **easily**.
4 Our trips are **better** than the trips offered by most other companies.
5 We look forward to **welcoming** you!
6 We are sure that you will want **to come** back again and again.

3 Peer pressure

Two weeks ago I found out that my friends went shoplifting. I was shocked. You see, I **hadn't done** anything like that before. But my friends laughed at me for **being** scared, and told me I **was** stupid. I **didn't want** to lose my friends, so last week I went into a shop with them and **stole** a scarf. But the following day the police came to my house and said they **had seen** me on CCTV. It was terrible. I **felt** I had lost my parents' respect, and I promised that I **would** never steal again.

4 Respect

0 Seretse Khama, who was the son of an African king, was studying in London in 1947.
1 **In 1948 Seretse married** a white English woman just one year after he had first met her.
2 After the wedding Ruth's father refused to speak with her because **she had married a black man**.
3 And the people in Seretse's country, called Botwana, didn't accept Ruth when she **arrived there**.
4 British people wouldn't accept a black queen, **so why should they accept** Ruth, they asked angrily.
5 But Ruth showed respect for them and soon **they respected** her and ignored her skin colour.
6 Amazingly this is a **true story that you can** see in a film called *United Kingdom*.

5 Applying for a job

0 Aisha Khan, who lives in York, is applying for a job today.
1 Aisha is still at school. She **has been at Haxby School since 2019**.
2 Before she began at Haxby School, **Aisha went to Primary School in York**.
3 Aisha **began Primary School in 2014**.
4 She **is interested in keeping fit**.
5 Aisha had experience of cleaning **when she worked for a cleaning company**.
6 Unfortunately, **Aisha didn't get the job**.
7 If she **had got the job, she would have been very happy**.

Meine Notizen

Titelbild

Illustration: Cornelsen/Dorina Tessmann

Illustrationen

Cornelsen/Karen Donnelly (**S. 6, 9, 11, 12, 16**)

Abbildungen

S. 6: stock.adobe.com/Mantis Design; **S. 11 ob.:** Shutterstock.com/grublee; **S. 17:** Shutterstock.com/BDLook; **S. 18:** Shutterstock.com/Nina Lishchuk; **S. 21:** Shutterstock.com/Tana888; **S. 26:** Shutterstock.com/sebra; **S. 27:** Shutterstock.com/Alice Day; **S. 28:** Shutterstock.com/studiostoks; **S. 29:** stock.adobe.com/Drobot Dean; **S. 30:** Shutterstock.com/Krakenimages.com; **S. 31:** Shutterstock.com/wavebreakmedia; **S. 33:** Shutterstock.com/Rawpixel.com; **S. 34 li.:** Shutterstock.com/simona pilolla 2; **re. :** Shutterstock.com/WAYHOME studio; **S. 36:** Shutterstock.com/Martin Charles Hatch; **S. 37:** Shutterstock.com/De Visu; **S. 38:** Shutterstock.com/Dina Lesnikova; **S. 41:** Shutterstock.com/AJR_photo; **S. 43:** Shutterstock.com/pictman.com; **S. 44:** Shutterstock.com/pathdoc